HISTORY THROUGH SOURCES

Russia and the USSR 1905–1956

NIGEL KELLY

Heinemann Library

Halley Court, Jordan Hill, Oxford OX2 8EJ
a division of Reed Educational & Professional
Publishing Ltd

OXFORD MADRID ATHENS FLORENCE PRAGUE
CHICAGO PORTSMOUTH NH (USA) MEXICO CITY
SAO PAULO SINGAPORE KUALA LUMPUR TOKYO
MELBOURNE AUCKLAND IBADAN NAIROBI
KAMPALA GABORONE JOHANNESBURG

First published 1996

00 99 98 97 96
10 9 8 7 6 5 4 3 2 1

British Library Cataloguing in Publication data
is available from the British Library on request.

ISBN 0431 05780X (P/B 0431 057818) 947.84

Produced by Dennis Fairey & Associates Ltd
Illustrations by Arthur Phillips
Printed by Mateu Cromo in Spain
Cover design by Ron Kamen
The publishers would like to thank Dr Stephen Vickers
and Andy Harmsworth for their comments on the
original manuscript.

Acknowledgements

The publishers would like to thank the following for
permission to reproduce photographs:

Bettmann Archive: 51
Centre for the Study of Cartoons and Caricature: 57
Jean-Loup Charmet: 16 below
Edimedia: 61
Hoover Institute: 18, 20, 25, 36, 37, 42, 48, 53, 59
Hulton Deutsch: 27, 29 centre
David King: 5, 10, 14, 21, 26, 40, 44, 56
Mansell Collection: 46
Radio Times/Hulton: 39
Roy Miles Gallery, London: 43 below
Novosti: 6, 16 top, 23, 29 left, 43, 49
Society for Co-operation in Russian and Soviet Studies:
    29 right
Times Newspapers Limited/Michael Powers: 31
Topham Picture Library: 7

Details of written sources

In some sources the wording or sentence structure has
been simplified to ensure that the source is accessible.

N. Adeev, *Revolution in 1917: A Soviet Chronicle,*
London, 1923-7: 4.1B, 4.3L
Alexander Barmine, *One Who Survived*, Putnam, 1945: 5.4F
J. Brooman, *The Great War*, Longman, 1992: 3B
J. Brooman, *Stalin and the Soviet Union*, Longman, 1992: 7.1B
Meriel Buchanan, *Dissolution of an Empire*, John Murray,
    1937: 3C, 4.2H

Brian Catchpole, *A Map History of Russia*, Heinemann, 1974: 2.1A
Deutscher and King, *The Great Purges*, Blackwell, 1984: 6.4X
M.T. Florinsky, *The End of the Russian Empire*, Putnam, 1971:
    3.1/1
David Floyd, 'Russia 1905-12', *History of the Twentieth Century*,
    Purnell, 1974: 2.5 6
Peter Gilliard, *Thirteen Years at the Russian Court*, London,
    1921: 2.4H
Eugenia Ginsburg, *Into the Whirlwind*, Collins, 1981: 6.4W
Joan Hasler, *The Making of Russia*, Longman, 1968: 7.1C
G. Katkov, *Russia 1917*, Longman, 1967: 3.1/7
Alexander Kerensky, *The Catastrophe*, New York, 1927: 4.2A
Alexander Kerensky, *Russia and History's Turning Point*,
    1965: 1.1D
John Laver, *Lenin, Liberator or Oppressor?*, 1994: 5.6/6/7
Letters of the Tsarina to the Tsar, 1914-16, introduction
    by Sir Bernard Pares, London, 1923: 2.4I, 4.1A
Lenin, Vladimir Ilich, *Collected Works*, Vols. 44 and 45,
    Lawrence and Wishart, 1970: 5.3B, 5.4J
Lenin, Vladimir Ilich, *Testament*: 6.1B, 6.1C
R. Medvedev, *Khrushchev*, 1982: 7.1E
Brian Moynahan, *The Russian Century*, Random House,
    1984: 5.4K
New York Tribune, December 1918: 4.5/5
J.E. O'Connor, *The Sokolov Investigation*, Souvenir Press,
    1972: 4.5/2/3/4
Richard Pipes, *The Russian Revolution 1899-1918*,
    Collins Harvill, 1990: 2.4G, 3.1/2, 5.2A
John Robottom, *Russia in Change 1870-1945*, Longman,
    1984: 6.3L, 7.3/3
J. Scott, *Behind the Urals*, Houghton Mifflin, 1942: 6.2K
Alexander Solzhenitsyn, *The Gulag Archipelago*,
    Harvill Press, 1974: 6.2I
Stalin, Josef, *History of the Communist Party of the Soviet Union*,
    1939: 6.4T
Stalin, Josef, *Selected Writings*, Greenwood Press,
    1942: 6.2E, F, 6.3N
M. Szeftel, *The Russian Constitution of April 23, 1906*,
    Brussels, 1976: 2.4D
The Times, 10 July, 1993: 4.5/7
Trotsky, Leon, *History of the Russian Revolution*, Pluto,
    1977: 5.4E, 5.4G
Trotsky, Leon, *My Life: An attempt at an Autobiography*,
    Pathfinder, 1970: 4.3J
Alan White, *Russia and the USSR*, Collins, 1994: 6.3P
de Witte, Sergei, *Memoirs of Count de Witte*,
    edited by Abraham Yarmolinsky, London, 1921: 2.4E
R.E. Zelnik, translator, *A Radical Worker in Tsarist Russia*,
    1986: 1.1B

CONTENTS

CHAPTER 1

RUSSIA UNDER THE TSAR

1.1 What was Russia like in 1905?

At the beginning of the twentieth century the Russian Empire (more usually known as Russia) covered one sixth of the world's surface. It was ruled by the **Tsar**, who was said to derive his power directly from God. Russia was not a wealthy country. The Tsar's family and the rich, landowning **nobles** lived a life of luxury. However, most of the people were **peasants** or factory workers, who were extremely poor. Opposition to the Tsar was growing.

▼ The Russian Empire in 1905.

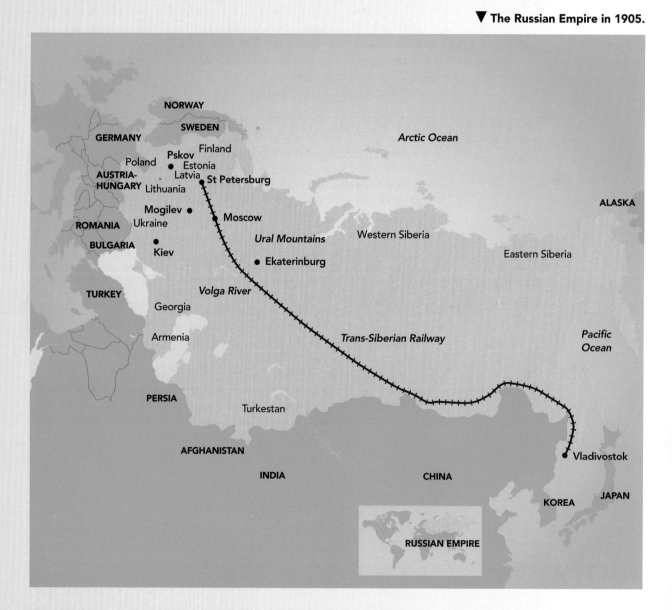

◀ A Russian village in about 1900.

A huge Empire

In 1905 Russia was almost one hundred times the size of Britain. It stretched from Europe in the west to the Pacific Ocean in the east, from the Arctic Ocean in the north to Persia and Afghanistan in the south. Its size made it appallingly difficult to govern. Roads were often impassable and even by the new **Trans-Siberian Railway**, it took weeks to cross the country.

An ungovernable people?

Russia had a wide variety of climates. In the north it was so cold that rivers and the Arctic Ocean often froze for long periods in the winter. Yet in parts of the south it was warm enough to grow cotton and grapes. The Russian people had a variety of different life styles to suit these climates. Of the 125,000,000 people living in the Russian Empire less than half were Russians. There were large numbers of Ukranians and Poles as well as people of over 100 different nationalities. These people spoke different languages and had different religions and cultures. To imagine that the Russian Empire was one united country would be wrong. It was a collection of very different people ruled by the same leader, many of them wishing to govern themselves.

Life in the countryside

At the beginning of the twentieth century more than three-quarters of the Russian population were peasants. Much of Russia's agricultural land was of poor quality and the peasants lived a hard life trying to feed the growing population. Food shortages were common and during times of severe famine, as in the winter of 1891–2, millions died of starvation.

B

I lived near the factory, in a large smelly house inhabited by all kinds of poor people. About fifteen of us rented one apartment. I was in a dark, windowless corner room. It was dirty and stuffy, full of bedbugs and fleas. There was just room for two wooden beds. I shared mine with one other man. The rooms stank of the mud from the streets, which was made up of dirt, rubbish and sewage.

▲ S.I. Kanatchikov recalls his life as a factory worker in Moscow in 1900.

Life in the towns

Industrial workers in Russia's main towns, such as St. Petersburg, also had a tough life. A normal working day was more than eleven hours and wages were very low. Because **trade unions** were banned and strikes were illegal, it was very difficult for workers to improve their conditions of employment. A shortage of housing meant that many factory workers were forced to live in accommodation provided by the employers. Here overcrowding was common and as many as ten people might live in one room, taking it in turns to sleep up to four at a time in one bed.

Of course not all Russians were poor. The nobles, although they made up only a tiny percentage of the Russian population, were both wealthy and highly influential. They owned a quarter of the land in Russia and lived a life of luxury, with large numbers of servants. There were also other wealthy Russians. These were the **capitalists**. They used their money (capital) to set up banks and factories or to develop trade. With wages low and little money spent on improving the conditions for workers, the capitalists were able to make excellent profits in early twentieth century Russia.

Running the country

In 1905 Russia was ruled by **Tsar Nicholas II**. He was an **autocrat**; he had all the power. He decided everything relating to Russia's government, economy, foreign relations and military forces. The people of Russia, including the peasants and town workers, (95% of Russia's population) had no say in the running of the country. Peasants lived in villages run by *mirs* (local councils), but the *mirs* had to do what the government said. Nicholas received advice from a **Committee of Ministers** – chosen from the nobility by the Tsar. To ensure that the Tsar's authority was not challenged, the **Okhrana**, (state police) kept a careful eye on potential opposition. Newspapers and books were censored and and those found guilty of political opposition to the Tsar usually ended up in exile in bleak and isolated Siberia.

Source **C**

▶ A political cartoon about Russian society, drawn around 1900. The workers at the bottom protest at their lack of freedoms. Next, the capitalists say 'We do the eating'; the army say 'We shoot you'; the clergy say 'we fool you'; and the nobles say 'We govern you'. The royal family at the top say 'We rule you'.

The **Russian Orthodox Church**, which most people belonged to, taught respect for authority and loyalty to the Tsar. Priests said it was a sin to oppose the Tsar. The Church was a major landowner in Russia and its head was one of the Tsar's government ministers.

Nicholas was not an able leader. His father, **Alexander III**, had died unexpectedly in 1895, at the age of 48. Just two years before his death Alexander had called his son 'still absolutely a child, with infantile judgements'. When Nicholas heard of his father's death he asked his brother-in-law 'What am I to do? I am not prepared to be Tsar. I know nothing of the business of ruling.' During his reign Nicholas was to be dominated by his German wife, **Alexandra**, who encouraged him to defend his **absolute** (complete) powers against any calls for reform.

1.2 Who opposed the Tsar?

The majority of Russians believed that God had chosen the Tsar to rule over them and that they should respect and obey him. They believed everyone had a place in society, and that they should accept their place and get on with living their lives as best they could. The Tsar, the nobles and the Church encouraged them to believe this.

However, not everyone believed that the Tsar's rule should go unchallenged. Some people looked at the wretched lives of the peasants and factory workers and demanded that something should be done to bring about improvements. Other people realized that the Tsar's autocratic rule was not the only way to govern. Economic development in Russia had brought greater contact with the West. People saw that countries like Britain and France were governed in a more democratic way. The people in these countries had a say in the way their country was run.

Nicholas's grandfather, Alexander II, had been assassinated in 1881. Both Nicholas' father, Alexander III, and Nicholas feared the same end. They made extensive use of the Okhrana to arrest and exile thousands of opponents of the government. Despite the fact that opposition was illegal there were still important groups of opposition in Russia. These groups were:

Source E

▲ The future Tsar Nicholas II in 1894.

1 The Liberals

The **Liberals** were the most moderate of Nicholas's opponents. They did not try to overthrow the Tsar, but instead wanted the Tsar to share his power by introducing western democratic ideas so that Russia had democracy and an elected parliament (**Duma**). The Liberals came mostly from the educated, professional classes and their major concern was that the Russian army and economy should keep up with the other great powers.

2 The Social Revolutionary Party

This party was formed in 1901. Its members believed that land should be shared by the peasants who farmed it, not owned by wealthy landowners. The party was prepared to take violent action – between 1890 and 1905 they killed a number of government officials, including Nicholas's uncle, Grand Duke, Sergei Aleksandrovich. The **Social Revolutionaries** hoped that the peasants could be organized to revolt against the Tsar.

3 The Social Democratic Party

The **Social Democrats** also wanted a revolution. The party's views were based on the writings of a German political thinker, Karl Marx. Marx wrote the *Communist Manifesto* in 1848, telling the workers to take control of factories and other '**means of production**'. These should be shared out equally among the citizens of Russia. Such a system was called socialism. Marx argued that, once socialism was established, the workers would develop an even better system, called communism. They would all work to produce goods that would then be shared. Everyone would get what they needed. Unfortunately, there was disagreement over how the revolution was to occur. In 1903 the Social Democrats split into two opposing groups: the **Mensheviks** and the **Bolsheviks**, led by **Lenin**. The Bolsheviks said the party should be run by an elite of dedicated revolutionaries. Mensheviks believed that power should be spread among as many members as possible. It was Lenin and the Bolsheviks who were to bring about the Communist Revolution of November 1917 (see page 28).

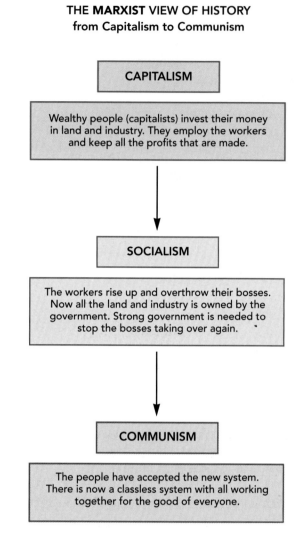

THE **MARXIST** VIEW OF HISTORY
from Capitalism to Communism

CAPITALISM

Wealthy people (capitalists) invest their money in land and industry. They employ the workers and keep all the profits that are made.

SOCIALISM

The workers rise up and overthrow their bosses. Now all the land and industry is owned by the government. Strong government is needed to stop the bosses taking over again.

COMMUNISM

The people have accepted the new system. There is now a classless system with all working together for the good of everyone.

KARL MARX (1818–33)

Karl Marx was born in Trier in Germany. He attended universities in Berlin and Bonn and wrote radical works such as the *Communist Manifesto*, which encouraged workers to overthrow their rulers, and *Das Kapital*, which said that everyone should have an equal share of wealth and power. Marx died in England in 1833 and is buried in Highgate Cemetery, London.

SUMMARY

Russia in 1905

▶ An autocratic Tsar supported by the Church and a state police.

▶ A wealthy nobility but the majority of the population living in poverty.

▶ A population of various nationalities, but dominated by Russians.

▶ A country with an growing number of illegal groups opposing the Tsar.

CHAPTER 2

1905: THE YEAR OF CHANGE

2.1 Why was there a revolution in 1905?

By 1905 many Russians were prepared to take action to show how much they disapproved of the way the Tsar was running the country. Violent opposition frightened the Tsar into making concessions, but in the years after 1905 most of them were withdrawn. By 1917 discontent had risen to such a level that Nicholas was forced to **abdicate**.

The 1905 Revolution

In 1905 Nicholas faced a serious uprising against his rule which forced him to make concessions in order to maintain his control. There were several reasons for the outbreak of opposition.

In 1902 Social Revolutionaries shot dead the Minister of Interior, **Dimitri Sipiagin**. Tsar Nicholas chose **Viacheslev Plehve** as the new Minister. Plehve was very unpopular and caused even more opposition to the Tsar. He encouraged attacks on the Jews and helped the Okhrana in its policy of setting up illegal trade unions to trap workers who tried to join them. In July 1904 Plehve was also assassinated.

The most significant cause of unrest in Russia in 1905 was the **Russo-Japanese War**. In 1904 Russia and Japan went to war over control of Manchuria and Korea. The Tsar hoped that a quick and decisive victory would make his government more popular. However, the war was a disaster. The Russian army suffered a series of defeats. In May 1905 the Japanese destroyed the Russian fleet at Tsushima. This fleet had arrived there just one day earlier after sailing for seven months from the Baltic Sea! In September 1905 Russia accepted Japanese control of Korea and much of Manchuria in the Treaty of Portsmouth.

Source A

On 15 October 1904 the Russian Baltic Fleet had left its base on a mission to relieve the Russian garrison at Port Arthur. After one of the most extra-ordinary voyages in the history of naval warfare, it suffered total defeat. The Japanese fleet surprised the twenty-seven warships as they steamed through the Straits of Tsushima. The battle was over in ninety minutes. Only three Russian ships made their escape.

▲ B. Catchpole, *A Map History of Russia*, 1974.

▼ The Russo-Japanese War 1904–5.

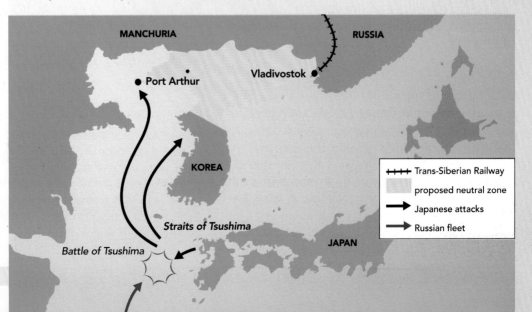

MANCHURIA   RUSSIA

● Port Arthur   Vladivostok ●

KOREA

Straits of Tsushima

JAPAN

Battle of Tsushima

┼┼┼┼ Trans-Siberian Railway
▢ proposed neutral zone
➤ Japanese attacks
➤ Russian fleet

Military defeats, coupled with disruptions to food supplies meant the Russo-Japanese war made the Tsar's government even more unpopular. On 22 January 1905, **Father Gapon** led 200,000 workers through the streets of St. Petersburg to the Tsar's **Winter Palace** to present the Tsar with a list of grievances. (The marchers did not know that the Tsar was not in the city at the time.) Troops, panicked by the size of the crowd, opened fire on the marchers. Official figures said 96 were killed and 333 wounded. The actual figures are probably much higher and the event became known in Russian history as Bloody Sunday.

▲ A cartoon from 1905. The skeleton-like figure is a revolutionary.

2.2 What happened after Bloody Sunday?

The events of 22 January shocked Russians and foreigners alike. In Britain, the Labour politician Ramsey MacDonald called the Tsar 'a blood-stained creature'. In Russia there was a wave of protests. More than half a million workers went on strike. On 17 February the Tsar's uncle, Grand Duke, Sergei Aleksandrovich, was assassinated. Nicholas was forced to agree to set up a 'consultative assembly' to discuss making political concessions.

Across Russia people began organizing themselves into unions to protect their rights. These unions were formed not just by industrial workers, but also by groups that had never before been organized, such as engineers, teachers and lawyers. In May 1905 the unions joined together to form the **Union of Unions**.

In the countryside peasants rose up, seized local land and murdered their landlords. The **minority nationalities** of Russia also rebelled. The Tsar had been following a policy of **'Russification'** which forced other peoples in the Empire (such as Poles and Armenians) to learn Russian and neglect their own cultures. The unrest in Russia which followed Bloody Sunday gave these peoples a chance to revolt against their Russian masters.

In June 1905, in Odessa, the crew of the **battleship** *Potemkin* mutinied in support of striking workers. The army moved in. About 2,000 people were killed and another 3,000 injured in putting down the mutiny. In September a printers' strike in St. Petersburg grew into a general strike which crippled Russia's communications and shut down its factories, shops and schools. The 200,000 workers chose 500 delegates to form a council or **Soviet** to organize the strikes in the city. Similar Soviets were elected in towns and cities across Russia. The Tsar's government was being replaced in many places by elected representatives of the people. The opposition to the Tsar at this time was so serious that historians usually refer to these events as the 1905 Revolution.

GEORGY GAPON (1870–1906)

Father Gapon was a priest from the Ukraine. Although he led the marchers on Bloody Sunday, he is believed to have been a police informer. After Bloody Sunday he fell out with the Tsar's government and went into exile. When he returned he was captured by the Social Revolutionaries, who accused him of being a police spy and hanged him in 1906.

The October Manifesto

Despite the violence and opposition to the Tsar in Russia in 1905, Nicholas survived the crisis and his authority was restored. Much of the credit for this lies with **Sergei Witte**, Nicholas's Chief Minister in 1905. He persuaded the Tsar to make concessions to the Liberals in Russia to win their support. Then the revolutionaries could be dealt with in a much harsher manner. Consequently, on October 17, 1905, Nicholas issued the October Manifesto setting out political rights for the people of Russia and agreeing to the setting up of an elected parliament – a **Duma**.

Reprisals

As the government re-asserted its control, its supporters were prepared to come more into the open. Office-holders, landlords and churchmen in particular had great loyalty to the Tsar. Many of them now formed organizations called Black Hundreds which carried out acts of reprisal against those who had opposed the Tsar. Thousands of opponents of the Tsar were murdered. The police and army stood by and let it happen.

A Duma was to be elected in Russia.

All Russian men had the right to vote.

All laws made in Russia had to be approved by the Duma.

The Russian people were to have the right to form political parties, have freedom of speech and hold meetings as they liked.

◀ **Concessions made by the Tsar in the October Manifesto.**

Source C

The publication of the October Manifesto was greeted with delight in Russia. The **St. Petersburg Soviet** called off the general strike and strikers in other cities also went back to work. Some revolutionaries warned that Nicholas could not be trusted to keep his word and that punishments would soon follow for opposition to the Tsar. They were soon proved right. The leaders of the St. Petersburg Soviet were arrested and exiled. When the **Moscow Soviet** organized an uprising at the end of 1905, the army crushed it in a battle which cost over a thousand lives. Peasants involved in burning their landlords' farms were hanged and the Tsar's authority was restored in non-Russian parts of the Empire, though often with great difficulty.

▲ **A modern historian commenting on how the Tsar soon restored his control after the October Manifesto was published.**

WITTE (1845-1915)

Sergei Witte was the first Russian prime minister. Although he attempted to give the Tzar good advice, it was rarely taken.

The Dumas

In the October Manifesto of 1905 Nicholas promised political rights and a Duma which would share in running the country. In the years immediately after 1905 he made sure neither of these things would happen.

In March 1906 the elections for the first Duma were held. The system of voting favoured landowners over peasants and workers. Even so, the majority of those elected were critics of the government. However, Nicholas ensured that the Duma would have little authority. In May he issued a set of **Fundamental Laws** which gave him total control over the Duma. He alone could make laws in Russia. He could dissolve the Duma, or change the laws by which it was elected, any time he liked.

The Duma first met in May 1906. When it demanded the right to appoint ministers and to have a greater say in government, Nicholas sent his troops to dissolve it. Russia's new parliament had lasted just over two months. A second Duma was elected in 1907. This lasted just five months before Nicholas dissolved it for criticizing his handling of the army. Nicholas then changed the voting system to ensure that the third Duma was less critical of his government. The richest one per cent of Russian citizens elected two-thirds of the representatives. Not suprisingly, Nicholas had little trouble from this Duma which lasted the full five years it was allowed to run. The fourth Duma, elected in 1912, also obeyed him.

Repression and reform

Nicholas regretted signing the October Manifesto and in 1906 dismissed Witte, who he blamed for having talked him into making concessions. The concessions made seemed to have done little good, because in early 1906 the Social Revolutionaries began a campaign of terrorism in which thousands of Russians were killed or injured. They wanted to show that the Tsar's government could not keep law and order in Russia.

Nicholas's solution was to appoint the hard-line **Peter Stolypin** as Chief Minister in July 1906. Stolypin promised that he would bring 'repression and reform'.

Source D

The Tsar alone may make laws in Russia.

The Tsar alone is in control of foreign affairs.

The Tsar alone is responsible for military matters.

All Ministers are appointed and dismissed by the Tsar alone.

The Tsar may dissolve the Duma whenever he chooses.

The system for electing the Duma is the responsibility of the Tsar alone.

▲ Some of the Fundamental Laws issued by Nicholas in 1906.

Source E

We talked for two solid hours. He shook my hand. He wished me all the luck in the world. I went home beside myself with happiness and found a written order for my dismissal lying on my desk.

▲ Sergei Witte describes his dismissal in 1906.

SUMMARY

Russia after Bloody Sunday

▶ **1905** Tsar made concessions in the October Manifesto.

Black Hundreds attacked Tsar's opponents.

▶ **1906** First Duma met and was dissolved. Tsar changed system of voting.

Stolypin introduced 'Repression and Reform'.

Revolutionary activity died down.

Repression

Stolypin immediately set up special courts called 'Field Courts for Civilians'. These provided rapid trials for those who were 'obviously guilty'. The accused could call witnesses, but were bound to be found guilty and had no right to appeal against the sentence of exile or execution. By the end of 1906 over a thousand alleged terrorists had been tried and executed. A further 20,000 revolutionaries were sent into exile in Siberia. So tough were Stolypin's measures that Russians nicknamed the hangman's noose 'Stolypin's necktie'. His measures were very successful. Execution, exile and flight abroad reduced the estimated numbers of revolutionaries in Russia from 100,000 in 1905 to 10,000 in 1910.

Reform

Stolypin also tried to reduce opposition to the Tsar by introducing reforms to help the peasants. He argued that if the Russian peasants had a higher standard of living, they would be less likely to support the revolutionary groups. So Stolypin encouraged the peasants to buy land from their local village commune (*mir*) which had owned it since the peasants were freed from serfdom in 1861. The government provided loans to help peasants buy land and by 1914 over two million peasants owned their land. However, only the wealthier peasants could afford to buy enough land to ensure that their families could be supported by their share, and many peasants continued to struggle to make ends meet. Farming continued to be highly inefficent in Russia. Peasants produced far fewer crops per acre than in Britain or other western countries. Stolypin's tough measures meant that there was less unrest in the factories and mines and so there were fewer strikes. In the period immediately after 1905 there was an increase in Russia's industrial production, though this declined after 1912 when industrial unrest broke out again.

▼ Russian industrial production 1900–14.

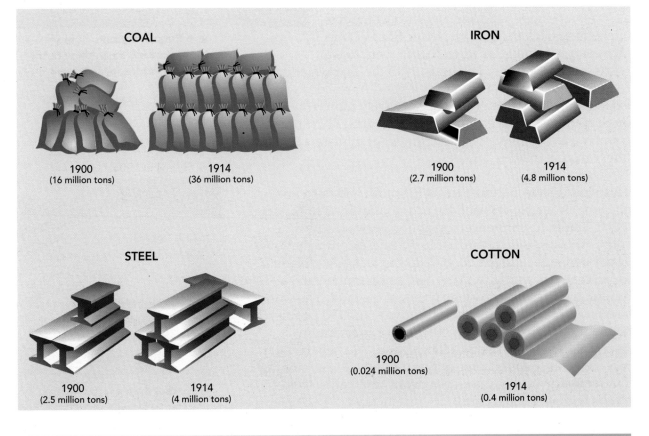

COAL
1900 (16 million tons)
1914 (36 million tons)

IRON
1900 (2.7 million tons)
1914 (4.8 million tons)

STEEL
1900 (2.5 million tons)
1914 (4 million tons)

COTTON
1900 (0.024 million tons)
1914 (0.4 million tons)

Rasputin

Stolypin's work had restored the Tsar's authority and quietened the revolutionary activity. However, events at the Tsar's court from 1911 soon helped stir up anti-government feeling once more. In September 1911 Stolypin was assassinated while attending the opera. Even before his death Stolypin's authority at court was being challenged by **Grigory Rasputin**. Indeed there were rumours that Stolypin was murdered by the Okhrana because he criticized Rasputin.

Rasputin, a peasant who called himself a holy man, came to the royal court in 1905. Nicholas's son, **Alexei**, suffered from a rare illness called **haemophilia**. This meant that his blood did not clot, and whenever he cut himself he was in danger of bleeding to death. Doctors could not cure the illness. Rasputin seemed to be able to calm the boy and on several occasions managed to stem internal bleeding. Obviously the royal family was delighted by Rasputin's success and he became highly influential at court.

Rasputin's influence at court owed much to Nicholas's wife, the Tsarina, Alexandra. She was a German princess who had always encouraged Nicholas to cling to absolute power. She became increasingly unpopular when Russia went to war with Germany in 1914. In August 1915 the Tsar went to the front to take command of the armies and Alexandra was left isolated in St. Petersburg. She began to rely more and more on Rasputin for advice and soon he was virtually running the country. He approved the appointment of ministers and even intervened in military affairs.

This would have mattered less if Rasputin had been an efficient leader. He was not. He had no idea how to conduct a war. Under his influence, corruption grew steadily at court. Able ministers were dismissed and incompetent ones appointed in their place. Soon Rasputin was being blamed for all that was wrong with the Tsar's government even though many of the problems were not his fault. The war also brought food shortages in the towns and the people blamed Rasputin for this. Another factor in Rasputin's unpopularity was his personal behaviour. He believed that true repentance could come only if it followed true sinning! Consequently he was often seen drunk and had scores of affairs with women at court.

▲ A Russian cartoon, published in 1916, showing Rasputin with the Tsar and Tsarina in each hand.

Truly you ought to be my eyes and ears there in the capital, while I have to stay here. It rests on you to keep peace and harmony among the ministers – thereby you do a great service to me and our country.

▲ Extract from a letter written by the Tsar to his wife in 1915.

Members of the royal family begged Alexandra to dismiss Rasputin, but she believed that his advice was indispensable and said: 'guided by him we will get through this heavy time'. In desperation, a group of noblemen led by Prince Yusupov took matters into their own hands and in December 1916 assassinated Rasputin. It was not an easy job getting rid of him. He was poisoned, shot and finally bound and pushed into an icy river where he drowned.

Rasputin's influence had been removed from government, but it had done untold harm to Russia. In the Tsar's absence government had been inefficient and corrupt and Rasputin's advice on how to fight the war had brought further military disasters. Most importantly, however, the Tsar's authority had been undermined. Nicholas had handed power over to his wife while he went to fight the war. She was unpopular both because she was German and because of her strongly autocratic views. To make matters even worse she had let an immoral so-called holy man bring Russia to the point of chaos. More and more Russians came to believe that the Tsar had to go.

Source H

There was nothing the Tsarina would not do for those she loved. Persuaded, as she was, that Rasputin was God's chosen one (had she not seen God answer his prayers when her son was ill?) she was convinced that he could use his powers to keep the Tsar in power and to keep her son alive. She thought that without him they were lost.

▲ Peter Gilliard, tutor to Nicholas and Alexandra's son Alexei, talking about the hold Rasputin had over the royal family.

Source I

Now before I forget I must give you a message from our friend, prompted by what he saw in his dreams last night. He begs you to order that one should advance near Riga. He says that it is necessary, otherwise the Germans will settle down so firmly for the winter that it will cost endless lives and trouble to make them move.

▲ Extract from a letter from the Tsarina to the Tsar in 1915. The 'our friend' referred to is Rasputin.

▼Rasputin after his murder in 1916.

Source J

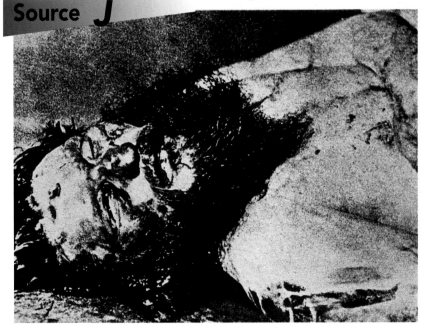

ALEXANDRA (1872–1918?)

Tsarina Alexandra was born Princess Alix of Hesse-Damstadt. She was the granddaughter of Queen Victoria. She married Nicholas in 1892 and was a strong supporter of his absolute rule. Whilst Nicholas was fighting in the war, Alexandra gave authority to Gregori Rasputin. This made the Tsar's rule even more unpopular. Alexandra, with her husband and most of her family, was probably shot in the Ipatiev House in 1918.

Source 1

▲ A photograph of Bloody Sunday.

Source 2

Sire

We workers and inhabitants of St. Petersburg come to thee to seek truth and defence.

We come as beggars; we have been oppressed, we are seen not as human beings, but as slaves who must endure their bitter fate in silence. Death is better than the continuation of intolerable tortures.

Our first request was that our masters should discuss our needs with us, but this was refused on the grounds that we have no right to make such a request. They also declared to be illegal our requests to reduce the working day to eight hours, to increase the minumum daily wage to one rouble, to abolish overtime, to provide medical attention without insulting us and to arrange the workshops so that it might be possible to work there and not find death in them from awful draughts and from rain and snow.

All these requests our employers described as illegal. Every one was a crime and the desire to improve our condition was regarded by them as impertinence and offensive.

▲ Extracts from the petition taken to the Winter Palace on Bloody Sunday.

Source 3

▲ A French picture drawn shortly after Bloody Sunday.

Source 4

▲ A German cartoon of 1905 showing the events of Bloody Sunday.

Source 5

22 January 1905
A painful day! There have been serious disorders in St. Petersburg because workers wanted to come up to the Winter Palace. Troops had to open fire in several places in the city. There were many killed and wounded. God, how painful and sad! Mama arrived from town, straight to Mass. I lunched with all the others. Went for a walk, with Misha. Mama stayed overnight.

▲ Extract from the diary of Tsar Nicholas II.

Source 6

Whole families joined in the processions. As they marched they sang hymns and the anthem 'God Save the Tsar'. They carried religious pictures and pictures of the Tsar. Long before they reached Palace Square, the separate columns of marchers were met by Cossacks [mounted soldiers] and foot soldiers. Once stopped they were ordered to disperse. When they failed to do so, the soldiers fired into the defenceless crowd of men, women and children. Within minutes hundreds were dead (the official figure is too low) and many more were injured.

▲ From David Floyd, 'Russia 1905-12', *History of the Twentieth Century*.

What happened on Bloody Sunday?

One of the most exciting activities in the study of history involves piecing together the story of an event from a series of sources with slightly different views or opinions.

The events of Bloody Sunday are a good example of such an exercise. Source 6 creates the impression of a violent attack on peaceful marchers with little apparent justification. This is reinforced by the two foreign pictures in Sources 3 and 4. However, the image of peaceful innocence is not quite so obvious in the photograph in Source 1. Historians would want to consider just how reliable the two drawings are and to what extent the photograph is truly representative of what happened on the day.

It is interesting to note that whilst Nicholas describes the events as a 'sad day' in his diary, the events receive only a little more attention than the arrival of 'Mama' for lunch.

CHAPTER 3

THE IMPACT OF THE FIRST WORLD WAR

In August 1914 Russia joined Britain and France in fighting the combined forces of Germany, Austria-Hungary and from October, Turkey. At first there was support for the war in Russia. Such was the strength of anti-German feeling that Nicholas changed the name of the capital, St. Petersburg, to Petrograd because St. Petersburg sounded too German.

In the first few weeks of the war two Russian armies advanced rapidly into East Prussia and Austria. Russian victory, however, was shortlived. The Germans called Field Marshall von Hindenburg out of retirement. He moved troops from the Western Front to fight in East Prussia. Within weeks his troops had won two massive victories over the Russians. At Tannenberg the Germans trapped the Russian troops in swampland. About 90,000 Russians were captured and over 100,000 drowned. The Russian general, Samsonov, committed suicide after the defeat. Just one week later the Germans slaughtered a further 100,000 Russian troops at the battle of Masurian Lakes.

By the end of 1914 the Russian army had lost over 1,000,000 men. In the spring of 1915 the Germans and Austrians invaded Russia and advanced over 300 miles. Nicholas dismissed his commander-in-chief and took command himself. This was a serious mistake. Before this the Russian people had blamed the Tsar's ministers and generals for the slaughter. Now Nicholas had to take the blame. In February 1916 he ordered an attack on the Germans which failed. There were heavy Russian casualties. In June 1916 General Brusilov launched a Russian offensive deep into Austria but was forced to retreat yet again. Over a million Russians died in this campaign alone. Morale was so low that another million deserted the fighting and returned home. The Tsar's decision to go to the front was also a mistake because he put Alexandra in charge. In effect, this meant that Rasputin was in control. They made such a poor job of governing Russia that the Tsar's government lost the support of the Russian people.

Source A

▲ A Russian First World War poster. The might of Russia (the medieval Russian knight) attacks a three headed monster. One head (Austria) is cut off. Another head (Germany) has been wounded.

Source B

The sight of thousands of Russians driven into two huge lakes or swamps to drown was ghastly. There were thousands of men, with their guns, horses and ammunition, struggling in the water. To shorten their agony, our men turned their machine guns on them.

▲ The German general, von Moltke, describes how the Germans slaughtered the Russian troops at Tannenberg.

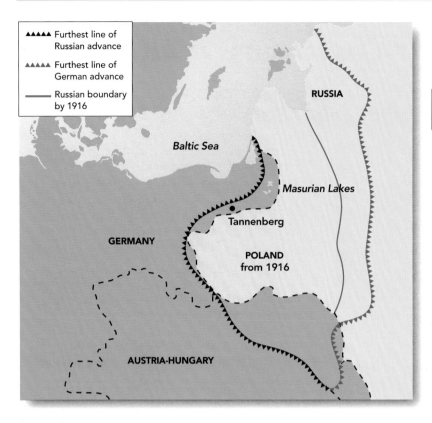

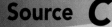
The Eastern Front 1914–17.

Key:
- ▲▲▲▲▲ Furthest line of Russian advance
- ▲▲▲▲▲ Furthest line of German advance
- —— Russian boundary by 1916

RUSSIA

Baltic Sea

Masurian Lakes

Tannenberg

GERMANY

POLAND from 1916

AUSTRIA-HUNGARY

Source C

The procession in the streets carrying the Tsar's portrait, framed in the flags of the Allies, the bands everywhere playing the national anthem. There was a long line of khaki-clad figures who marched away, singing and cheering; tall, bronzed men with honest, open faces, with childlike eyes, and a trusting faith in the Tsar – and a sure and certain hope that the saints would protect them and bring them safely back to their villages.

▲ Meriel Buchanan, whose father was the British Ambassador in St. Petersburg from 1910–1918. She is describing the Russian army leaving for war, August 1914.

The war had a devastating effect on the Russian economy. Inflation increased so that prices went up seven times between 1913 and 1917. The huge numbers of men fighting in the war meant that there was a shortage of labour to cultivate the land. It has been estimated that between a third and a half of peasant families had no male to help work on the land. The demand for horses at the Front also made it harder for peasants to cultivate their land. Industry too was hit by a shortage of workers and, as the war dragged on, by lack of fuel and other essential supplies. Russia simply did not have the transport system to move huge numbers of soldiers, supply the people with food and keep the necessary raw materials arriving at the factory gates.

Source D

◄ The economic effect of the First World War on Russia.

	1914	1915	1916	1917
Men mobilized (millions)	6.5	11.2	14.2	15.1
% of working males in army	14.9	25.9	35.7	36.7
Grain production (in poods)*	3509	4006	3319	3185
Inflation (taking a 1913 rouble as 100)	130	155	300	755

* 1 pood = 18kgs

Source 1

The behaviour of the soldiers, especially in the units in the rear, is most provocative. They accuse the military authorities of corruption, cowardice, drunkenness, and even treason. Everywhere one meets thousands of deserters perpetrating crimes and offering violence to the civilian population. The civilians express their regret that the Germans did not arrive, because they would restore order.

▲ A Petrograd police report of army morale in October 1916.

Source 2

Again that cursed question of shortage of artillery and rifle ammunition. If we should have three days of serious fighting we might run out of ammunition altogether. Without new rifles it is impossible to fill the gaps. The army is now almost stronger than in peace time; it should be [and it was at the beginning] three times as strong.

▲ Extract from a letter from the Tsar to the Tsarina in July 1915.

Source 3

A total absence of patriotic feeling can be seen in the mood of the working masses. The high cost of living, exploitation, and the barbaric policy of the government has proved to the masses the true nature of the war. There is an increase in strikes throughout the country. Prices have gone up five to ten times compared with last year. Clothing and footwear are becoming unobtainable and you no longer talk about meat.

▲ A letter written by a revolutionary to Lenin, the leader of the Bolsheviks, in December 1916.

Source 4

Despite all the losses, at the start of 1917 Russia looked strong enough, as a military power, to fight on. The war economy was going full-blast, and the Russian generals were confident; at the war front they had more men, more guns, more ammunition than the enemy. They could look forward to a year of successful campaigning.

▲ Tony Howarth, *Twentieth Century History: the World Since 1900*, Longman, 1979.

▼ *'Everything for the War'*. A Russian poster encouraging women to work in munitions factories.

Source 5

◀ Russian prisoners of war under guard in May 1915.

Things are getting worse; the men are splendid, there are plenty of guns and ammunition, but there is a lack of grey matter in the generals' heads. We are ready to die for Russia, but not for the whim of a general.

▲ Extract from a letter home by an officer in the army in late 1916.

▲ An anti-war poster issued by the Bolsheviks during the war. It shows the Tsar, the Church and the Russian nobility riding on the shoulders of ordinary Russians.

Russia and the First World War

Some historians believe that the most important factor in bringing about the downfall of the Tsar's government was the effect of defeat in the First World War. Not only did Russian forces perform badly (after some early successes), but the war led to serious shortages and privation in the country at large.

Sources 2 and 3 emphasize the problems created by the war and the lack of support for the Tsar is highlighted in Source 1. In this source some Russian civilians claim that they would rather have lived under German rule, as law and order was more likely than under the Tsar. It is interesting to note, however, that the traditional story of defeat through shortages might not be the whole picture. Both Sources 4 and 7 show that supplies were not necessarily lacking, but that leadership was. Source 8 further illustrates the unpopularity of the war and shows how the Tsar's political opponents used Russia's poor showing to create propaganda.

CHAPTER 4

1917: THE YEAR OF REVOLUTIONS

NOTE ON DATES

At the beginning of 1917 Nicholas II was still Tsar of Russia. His government's inefficiency and the humiliation of continued defeat in the war made him extremely unpopular, but few can have expected the dramatic turn of events that occurred in 1917. By the end of the year the Tsar had been forced to **abdicate** following the **March Revolution**.
A further revolution in November swept from power the **Provisional Government**, which had taken over from the Tsar. From November 1917 Russia was governed by the Bolsheviks – who just a few months earlier had been living in exile, forced out by the Tsar's government.

In 1918 the Bolshevik government changed the Russian calendar. Before this, Russian dates were two weeks ahead of the rest of Europe. So the revolutions which took place in March and November in Russia took place in February and October in the rest of Europe. All dates in this book are based on the Russian calendar.

4.1 Why did the Tsar abdicate in March 1917?

The final overthrow of the Tsar happened more by chance than by any great plan. Indeed, some historians argue that the March Revolution broke out because of the severity of the Russian winter. The first three months of 1917 were much colder than usual, with temperatures averaging -12°C. The Russians were used to cold weather, but on top of food and fuel shortages due to the First World War, it was too much.

The revolution began in the capital, Petrograd. Dissatisfaction with the the Tsar's government, rising prices, food shortages and defeats in the war came to a head when the shops began to run out of bread. Women who had queued outside bakers' shops for hours were told there was no bread. The women attacked the bakeries. On the next day thousands of workers began protest strikes. Crowds gathered shouting anti-government slogans. On 9 March, 200,000 demonstraters gathered in the city centre and revolutionaries distributed leaflets calling for the overthrow of the government. Shops were attacked and buildings set on fire. The commander of the city's military forces, **General Khabolov**, was in a very difficult situation. The Tsar instructed him to stop the 'disorders in the capital which are now unacceptable', but Khabolov's men were new recruits, many of whom had great sympathy with the striking citizens – and they were also suffering from the shortages.

Source A

The strikers and rioters in the city are now in more defiant mood than ever. The whole trouble comes from these idlers, well-dressed people, wounded soldiers, high-school girls etc. They are running around saying that they have no bread: they do this just to create some excitement. But things will quiet and settle down. They say it is all different from 1905 because they all worship you and only want bread.

▲ Letter from the Tsarina Alexandra to Nicholas, 10 March 1917.

On 11 March troops fired on rioting strikers, although one company refused to do so and had to be replaced. On the same day the Duma told Nicholas, still at his war-time headquarters at Mogilev, that he must form a new government which had the support of the people. Nicholas did not understand the seriousness of the situation. He told General Voyeikov to dissolve the Duma. He also said, 'That fat **Rodzyanko** has again sent me some nonsense to which I will not even reply.'

By the end of the next day, 12 March, the capital was out of control. Troops refused to fire on strikers. Instead one regiment mutinied, killed its officers and joined in the demonstrations. Soon other soldiers also mutinied. Many handed over their weapons to the strikers. Petrograd's garrison was reduced from 34,000 to less than 2,000. The city was in the hands of revolutionaries.

The Tsar saw the seriousness of the situation too late. The train on which he was returning to Petrograd was stopped at Pskov. It was not safe to go further. On 15 March Nicholas **abdicated** in favour of his brother, the Grand Duke Michael. When Michael refused to become Tsar, the monarchy in Russia was finished.

The situation is serious. The capital is in a state of anarchy. The government is paralysed; the transport system is broken down; the food and fuel supplies are completely disorganized. Discontent is on the increase. There is wild shooting on the streets; troops are firing at each other.

▲ Telegram sent by Rodzyanko, President of the Duma, to the Tsar on 11 March 1917.

RODZYANKO (1859–1924)

Michael Rodzyanko, a wealthy landowner, was president of the Duma and helped set up the Provisional Government. He opposed the Bolshevik takeover of Russia and was forced to flee in 1920.

▼ Soldiers joining the revolution in Petrograd in March 1918.

The Duma met on 11 March, despite the order from the Tsar to end the session. Russia was in the middle of a revolution. But who would win? Should the Duma's representatives obey the Tsar or use the revolution to take power and bring about reform? At last they decided to form a 'Provisional Government' until elections could be held for a new parliament. The Provisional Government held a cross-section of political views. The new Prime Minister, **Prince Lvov**, was a noble. Most of the other members were Liberals. However, **Alexander Kerensky**, an important Social Revolutionary, was Minister of Justice.

The Petrograd Soviet

Kerensky's inclusion in the Provisional Government shows one of its major problems. During March 1917 the workers in Petrograd had formed a Soviet (workers' council) similar to the one formed during the 1905 Revolution. The Soviet, not the Provisional Government controlled Petrograd. The Soviet had 3,000 members, each representing up to a thousand workers or soldiers. The Provisional Government could not rule without its support. Kerensky, a leading member of the Soviet, was in the government to give the Soviet a voice. In the early months of its life the Provisional Government had the support of the Petrograd Soviet, but that support was short-lived.

The war drags on

The Provisional Government decided to continue the war. Many of its members believed that the war could be won and that victory would bring them support. Unfortunately, the new government was no more successful at war than the Tsar had been. A new offensive in the summer of 1917 was a terrible failure. There were further strikes and rioting in the streets. At the Front, soldiers deserted in their thousands. The longer the war dragged on, the more unpopular the government became.

Source D

It inherited nothing from the Tsar, but a terrible war, an acute food shortage, a paralysed transportation system, an empty treasury, and a population in a state of furious discontent and anarchic disintegration.

▲ Alexander Kerensky commenting on the Provisional Goverment's position in 1917.

Source E

1. In all companies, battalions, regiments, batteries, squadrons, and on the vessels of the navy, committees from elected representatives of the lower ranks shall be chosen immediately.

2. The orders of the Duma shall be executed only in such cases as do not conflict with the orders of the Soviet of Workers' and Soldiers' Deputies.

6. Standing at attention and compulsory saluting, when not on duty, is abolished.

7. Addressing of the officers with the title, 'Your Excellency', 'Your Honour' etc. is abolished and these titles are replaced by the address of 'Mister General' 'Mister Colonel' etc.

▲ Extracts from 'Military Order No. 1' issued by the Petrograd Soviet on 14 March 1917.

SUMMARY

▶ **9 March**
Major anti-government riots in Petrograd.

▶ **11 March**
Troops open fire on demonstrators.
Duma dissolved.

▶ **12 March**
Government loses control in Petrograd.
Troops desert or mutiny.

▶ **15 March**
Tsar Nicholas abdicates;
Provisional Government set up.

Not enough change?

Another problem faced by the Provisional Government was the high expectations created by the overthrow of the Tsar. Many Russians expected the government to introduce reforms immediately to improve their living standards. The peasants believed the land would be taken from the wealthy and redistributed so that everyone had a share. But the power of the Provisional Government was still shaky; it did not control the provinces. Its members had little experience of government, and few of them wanted radical reform. They decided to delay making important decisions until new elections were held in November. This frustrated many Russians who wanted much quicker reform.

The government did make some important changes. Political prisoners were freed. Freedom of speech and of the press were introduced. Unfortunately for the government one of the major effects of these reforms was that its political opponents could now make their voices heard more easily.

Source F

▲ A poster issued by the Provisional Government showing a Russian soldier backed by workers and soldiers in a heroic continuation of the war.

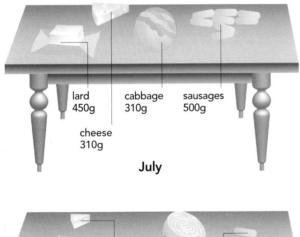

lard 450g   cabbage 310g   sausages 500g

cheese 310g

July

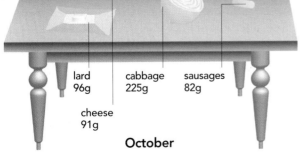

lard 96g   cabbage 225g   sausages 82g

cheese 91g

October

▲ Inflation in 1917. What a rouble could buy in July and October.

Source G

Men like me have got no guns behind us, it is hard to keep order. The new government in Petrograd does not give us any support. We only have two militia men to keep order in fifty villages. We should have at least fifty armed men, telephones, automobiles. As it is, the young hooligans steal horses and cattle and run riot. We can do nothing. We cannot even call for help if they set a house or a village on fire. They have broken into Prince C's house and stolen all his papers and wrecked the place.

▲ As reported to Ernest Poole, an American visitor, by the head of the local militia in a small village near Petrograd.

Returning revolutionaries

Among the government's political opponents were revolutionaries who had been in exile during the Tsar's reign. When the Tsar abdicated these people returned to Russia and immediately created further problems for the government. One such revolutionary was **Vladamir Ulyanov**, better known as **Lenin**. He was the leader of the Bolsheviks and wanted Russia to pull out of the war. The Germans supplied the Bolsheviks with funds. They even laid on a train to bring Lenin back to Russia from exile. They hoped he would persuade the government to end the war.

Lenin found the Bolsheviks had little influence in the government. His idea of world revolution giving complete power to the Soviets (which were springing up in Russian cities) also had little support. He had been away too long. He saw that he needed to get other Bolsheviks to agree with his ideas. Then the Bolsheviks had to convince the people of Russia to support them. All through 1917 Lenin and his main supporters, Stalin, Trotsky and Zinoviev, steadily spread their views. Talks were held in the factories and among the soldiers at the Front. Here Bolsheviks delivered Lenin's message, simplified into the slogan **Peace, Land and Bread**. The Bolshevik message was reinforced in their newspaper *Pravda* (Truth) which poured out propaganda against the government. As a result, support for the Bolsheviks grew rapidly.

▲ A painting of Lenin addressing the crowd at Finland Station in April 1917.

Source H

1 Desertions continue: Between 1 and 7 April, 7,688 soldiers deserted.

3 The authority of officers and commanders has collapsed.

5 Defeatist literature and propaganda has built itself a firm nest in the army.

▲ Extracts from the report of the War Minister, Alexander Guchkov, to the Provisional Government in April 1917.

KERENSKY (1881–1970)

Kerensky was born Alexander Fyodorovich in Simbirsk in 1881. By coincidence, Lenin was also born in Simbirsk and was taught at school by Kerensky's father.

Kerensky attended St. Petersburg University and graduated in law in 1904. He joined the Social Revolutionary Party in 1905. He was elected to the Duma in 1912 and in 1917 was made President of the Provisional Government. After the Provisional Government was ousted in the October Revolution, Kerensky left Petrograd, but failed to organize resistance to the Bolsheviks. He fled abroad to France and finally settled in the United States. There he wrote extensively about Russian history.

The July Days riots

Defeat on the battlefield in June 1917 increased the unpopularity of the government. Half a million workers went on strike in Petrograd. This unrest developed into what has become known as the **July Days** when soldiers, sailors and workers rioted in the city demanding an end to the war and the establishment of a Bolshevik government. The Bolsheviks had not planned the uprising. Lenin believed that his party was not yet ready for government. Kerensky (who replaced Prince Lvov as Prime Minister in July) acted swiftly. He arrested hundreds of Bolsheviks. He accused Lenin of being a German agent, publishing details of how the Germans had provided a train for Lenin to return to Russia. Lenin was forced to flee to Finland.

Kerensky then appointed **General Kornilov** as Supreme Commander of the Russian army. Kornilov was opposed to the changes being made in Russia. He tried to persuade Kerensky to reintroduce the death penalty for opposition to the government. Then, in September, he tried to overthrow the Provisional Government and set up a military **dictatorship** in Russia.

Kerensky was forced to release the Bolsheviks to help fight Kornilov and keep himself in power. Kornilov soon found that he did not have enough support. He was arrested by Kerensky's men.

4.3 How did the Bolsheviks seize power?

• •

By the autumn of 1917 the Provisional Government faced enormous difficulties. The war was going badly. The Russian people were faced with inflation and food shortages. There were rapidly increasing demands for immediate reform and the Bolsheviks were actively working for the overthrow of the government. Events were moving faster than the Bolsheviks planned.

Source J

We sent a detachment of sailors to the telephone exchange, and they placed two small guns at the entrance. The telephone girls fled with hysterical screams through the gates. The sailors managed somehow to handle the work of the switchboard. Thus began the taking over of the organs of administration. At the railway terminals, specially appointed Commissaries are watching the incoming and outgoing trains.

▲ Trotsky describes the events of 7 November 1917.

Source K

◄ The Women's Death Battalion, which defended the Winter Palace on 7-8 November.

Ready for action

The Bolsheviks, while fighting with Kerensky against Kornilov, had been given weapons. They won control of both the Petrograd and Moscow Soviets. In October 1917 Lenin ordered the Bolsheviks to prepare for a takeover of power. He returned to Petrograd (under heavy disguise to avoid arrest) where he and Trotsky planned to launch the revolution on 7 November, when the Congress of Soviets (a meeting of all the Soviets of Russia) was being held in the capital.

The Bolsheviks make their move

On 7 November the Bolsheviks moved the cruiser *Aurora* up the River Neva so that it was opposite the Winter Palace and seized control of strategic points in the city. The next morning, Lenin issued an announcement to the press that the Provisional Government had been deposed. It was ordered to surrender or face attack from the guns of the *Aurora*. After a token resistance, mostly by the 140 members of the Women's Death Battalion (originally formed to shame men into fighting in the war), the government surrendered. The Bolsheviks took control of the Winter Palace. The revolution resulted in just five deaths, but was to bring communist government to Russia for over seventy years. Prime Minister Kerensky escaped from Petrograd. He tried to raise fresh troops at the Front to oppose the Bolshevik takeover. The troops refused to support the Provisional Government. The Bolsheviks had finally taken control in Russia.

Source L

To the citizens of Russia

The Provisional Government is overthrown. Government authority has passed into the hands of the Petrograd Soviet of Workers' and Soldiers' Deputies. The cause for which the people have been fighting, namely the immediate offer of a democratic peace, the abolition of landed ownership, workers' control over production and the establishment of Soviet power – this cause has now been secured.

Long live the revolution of workers, soldiers and peasants!

▲ Extracts from posters announcing the Bolshevik revolution to the people of Petrograd, 8 November, 1917.

SAMOILOVA (1876–1921)

A great woman leader of the Bolshevik period, by 1912 Konkordiya Samoilova was editor of Pravda and in 1913 started the radical paper 'Woman Worker'.

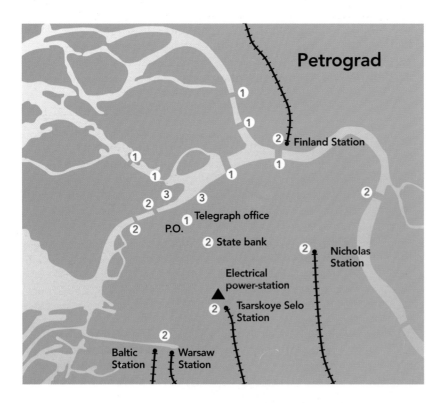

◀ The events of 7-8 November.

① **Early morning 7 November:** Red Guard take main bridges, P.O. and telegraph office

② **Day of 7 November:** railway stations taken, more bridges, electrical station and bank

③ **7–8 November:** St Peter and St Paul Fortress, Winter Palace taken

Vladimir Ulyanov
LENIN

Vladimir Ulyanov was born in Simbirsk, on the River Volga in 1870. His parents were both teachers and Lenin himself was a gifted and hard working pupil. In 1887 Lenin's brother, Alexander, was executed for involvement in a bomb plot against Alexander III. Lenin is said to have become determined to be a professional revolutionary from this date onwards. In 1887 he went to Kazan University to study law, but was expelled for revolutionary activity. In 1890 he enrolled at St. Petersburg University and graduated top of his year in law. He developed an interest in the writings of Karl Marx and smuggled his works into Russia after a visit to Europe in 1895. He was exiled to Siberia in 1897. From 1900–1917 he spent fifteen years abroad in exile. He returned to Russia in April 1917, after the March Revolution.

Joseph Djugashvili
STALIN

Stalin was born in 1879, the son of a Georgian bootmaker. His mother was determined that he would rise in the world. She worked hard to pay for his education. He worked well at school, but was expelled from college in 1899 for failing to take his exams. Already he was more concerned with the ideas of Karl Marx. He wanted to work for the revolution. He took part in over 1,000 raids to seize money in the period 1905–8. In 1907 Lenin wrote to Stalin saying that he was prepared to accept that Stalin changed his women 'as often as he changed his shirts', but did not want Stalin to organize brothels to raise money for revolutionary funds. Stalin spent much of the period 1905–17 either in exile in Siberia or on the run from the authorities in Russia. He was freed from exile in Siberia in 1917 and returned to Petrograd to become editor of the Bolshevik newspaper *Pravda*.

Lev Bronstein
TROTSKY

Trotsky was born in 1879 in a remote part of the southern Ukraine. He was the son of a Jewish farmer and was educated at Odessa University. While at university he became interested in the the writings of Karl Marx and began to write pamphlets and articles supporting revolutionary ideas. As a result he spent long periods in exile, both in Siberia and abroad. Unlike Stalin and Lenin, Trotsky was at first a Menshevik and did not join the Bolsheviks until 1917. This meant that those Bolsheviks who had been in the party for many years were suspicious of him. Trotsky returned to Petrograd from exile in May 1917 and played a major part in organizing the Bolshevik takeover in October.

4.5 What happened to the Romanovs after 1917?

1 The problem

After the Bolsheviks took power in November 1917, a civil war broke out between their supporters (the Reds) and those opposed to Bolshevism (the Whites). Some of the Whites wanted to restore the Tsar to power. The Bolsheviks took the Romanovs prisoner to prevent this. They arrived in Ekaterinburg in the remote Ural mountains on 30 April 1918. They were last seen alive on 16 July of that year.

The Romanovs' disappearance probably means that they were killed, but there is little firm evidence to prove this. In 1918 Judge Sergeyev, who opposed the Bolsheviks, investigated their disappearance. Between January and July 1919 another investigation was carried out by Judge Sokolov, a supporter of the Whites.

2 The evidence from the time

Source 1

Ekaterinburg was seriously threatened by the danger of an advance of White gangs, which had the object of snatching out of our hands the crowned hangman. We, the leaders of the Ural Soviet, decided to execute, by shooting, Nicholas Romanov, which was done on 16 July. The wife and son of Nicholas Romanov have been sent off to a secure place.

▲ **Statement published in 1918, by Bolsheviks in Moscow.**

Source 2

When I entered the room all were dead except for Alexei who was still moaning. Before my eyes Yurovsky gave him two or three shots with his revolver and he stopped moaning. I saw the following people dead. Nicholas, Alexandra, Alexei, his four daughters, Dr. Botkin, his cook, assistant and maid.

▲ **Extract from the testimony of Pavel Medevedev, a guard where the Romanovs were held at Ipatiev House, Ekaterinburg. It was given to Judge Sokolov.**

POINTS TO CONSIDER

1 Both investigations at the time were made by opponents of the Bolsheviks.

2 If other countries thought the Bolsheviks had executed the Romanovs, they might want to send troops to help the Whites.

3 If the Tsar was dead some Whites might see little point in continuing to fight.

4 Ekaterinburg was in the hands of the Reds on 16 July 1918, but was under threat from White forces, which finally captured the town on 25 July.

5 During the Civil War officers on both sides sometimes had to make decisions without contacting headquarters.

6 Between 1918 and 1987 the government of Russia never said what had happened to the Romanovs.

Source 3

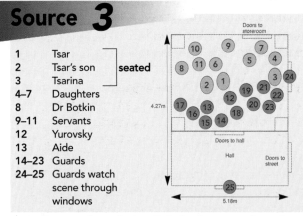

1	Tsar
2	Tsar's son
3	Tsarina
4–7	Daughters
8	Dr Botkin
9–11	Servants
12	Yurovsky
13	Aide
14–23	Guards
24–25	Guards watch scene through windows

▲ **A diagram from Judge Sokolov's report, based on witness interviews, of the death room.**

Source 4

Under the cover of darkness a lorry carried the corpses of the seven Romanovs and their servants to the Four Brother's mine. The bodies were chopped up, destroyed with sulphuric acid, and burnt on bonfires.

▲ **Part of the report by Judge Sokolov in 1919.**

Sergeyev said 'Here I have all the evidence in the Romanov case. I do not believe that all the people were shot in the Ipatiev House. It is my belief that the Tsarina, the Tsar's son, and the four other children were not shot in the house, but that the Tsar, his doctor, two servants and the maid were shot there.'

▲ An interview with Sergeyev printed in the *New York Tribune* in December, 1918.

3 The recent evidence

One of the consequences of the doubts over the fate of the Romanovs is that, since 1918, various people have claimed to be one of the family who escaped in 1918 and has been in hiding ever since. No one has claimed to be the Tsar or Tsarina, but in the 1920s people claimed to be one of the children, and as late as 1960 a defector from East Germany to the West claimed to be Alexei. One of the strongest claims was made in 1922 by a women called Anna Anderson who said that she was Anastasia. She said she had hidden behind her sisters during the massacre, and been rescued by a kindly Bolshevik soldier. Many people became convinced that she was telling the truth. In 1991 a collection of bones was found in a forest near Ekaterinburg. They were brought to Britain, where advances in forensic science, especially DNA sampling, made tests possible which provide almost certain proof of the authenticity of remains.

DNA tests identify Tsar's skeleton

British scientists have proved virtually beyond doubt that bones unearthed in eastern Russia in 1991 are those of the murdered Tsar Nicholas II and his family. They conclude that there is a 98.5 % probability that the bones are the Romanovs. Two members of the royal family remain unaccounted for; the Tsar's heir, Alexei and one of his daughters.

▲ Account from *The Times*, 10 July 1993.

▼ Photographs of Nicholas and Alexandra, together with the bones found at Ekaterinburg. From *The Times* 18 September 1993.

The Death of the Romanovs

One of the most fascinating problems for historians studying the events of the Revolution is to decide what happened to the Tsar and his family. In 1918, the Bolsheviks in Moscow claimed that the Tsar and his family had been executed. Other evidence suggested that they had been murdered and their bodies destroyed with acid. Yet in the 1920s a series of people claimed to be surviving members of the family.

In 1991 a collection of bones was found in Russia and DNA sampling suggested that the bones were the remains of the Tsar's family. The mystery appeared to have been solved – but there were two members of the family unaccounted for – Alexei and one of the Tsar's daughters. We still do not know what happened to them.

CHAPTER 5

LENIN AND THE ESTABLISHMENT OF THE USSR

In November 1917 the Bolsheviks seized power in Petrograd. They had two tasks. Firstly, they had to extend their authority to all parts of Russia. Secondly they had to make sure that supporters of the Tsar or the Provisional Government did not sweep them from power.

The years immediately following the November Revolution were difficult for the Bolsheviks. They had to get out of the First World War.

Their enemies in Russia joined under the White banner to fight them in a bloody civil war. The Whites were helped by foreign powers keen to topple the Bolsheviks. Victory was won, but at a high cost. The harshness of the regime the Bolsheviks had adopted to win the war lost them many of their strongest supporters. It was only by watering down its communist policies that Lenin's government could keep itself in power.

5.1 What problems did the Bolsheviks face in November 1917?

The Bolshevik take-over in November 1917 had been achieved with the minimum of bloodshed. But the new government was far from secure. The revolution had taken place too soon – the Army, the Soviets, the Party were not prepared. The first months of power were spent in a state of permanent crisis on all fronts. The Bolsheviks controlled Petrograd, but this was just a small part of the Russian Empire. Would the rest of the country accept the new government? One week after taking power the Bolsheviks captured Moscow. Lenin's government sent telegrams all over Russia explaining what had happened in Petrograd. In response, some areas, such as Finland, declared themselves independent of Russia. Most major towns and cities elected Soviets, but in some areas people resisted the Bolsheviks. It would take a bloody civil war lasting three years to win control of the whole country.

In Petrograd Lenin set up a temporary Council of People's Commissars (**Sovnarkom**). Most members of this government were Bolsheviks, but Lenin had to include some Mensheviks and Social Revolutionaries to ensure their support. They discussed policies, but in reality Lenin and his close advisers made the decisions. Bolshevik rule was by decrees issued by Prime Minister Lenin.

Others
162 seats

Bolsheviks
175 seats

Social Revolutionaries
370 seats

▲ The share of seats in the Constituent Assembly after the elections of November 1917.

The Provisional Government had arranged for a new parliament, the Constituent Assembly, to be elected in November 1917. Lenin stood by this arrangement. The result was an overwhelming victory for his political rivals the Social Revolutionaries. So when the Assembly met for the first time on 18 January 1918, Lenin sent troops to dissolve it.

Lenin also faced the problem of keeping the promises that he had made to the people.

The Bolshevik slogan of 'Peace, Land and Bread' had proved highly popular. Bolshevik supporters now expected to see the promises turned into reality. Lenin knew the Provisional Government had lost support by its failure to introduce reforms and to end the war. The Bolsheviks had to get Russia out of the war and help improve the lives of the urban and rural poor. It was important that they acted quickly.

5.2 How did Lenin ensure Bolshevik survival?

Although his government effectively controlled only a small part of Russia, Lenin immediately took steps to introduce reforms. He also changed the name of the Bolshevik party to the Communist Party and in 1918 decreed that the only party allowed in Russia was the Communist Party.

Ending the war
Lenin had hoped the German and Austrian governments would make peace without making excessive demands on Russia. He was to be disappointed. When the three countries met in the town of **Brest-Litovsk** in December 1917 it soon became obvious that Russia was going to have make huge concessions of land to buy peace.

Source A

- Negotiations for an end to the war will begin immediately.

- Land owned by the Tsar, the church and the nobility is to be redistributed.

- Religious teaching is to stop.

- Women are to be considered the equal of men.

- All titles, except 'Citizen' and 'Comrade' are abolished.

- Factory workers should work a maximum day of 8 hours.

- All non-Bolshevik newspapers are to be closed.

▲ Decrees issued by the Bolsheviks between November 1917 and March 1918.

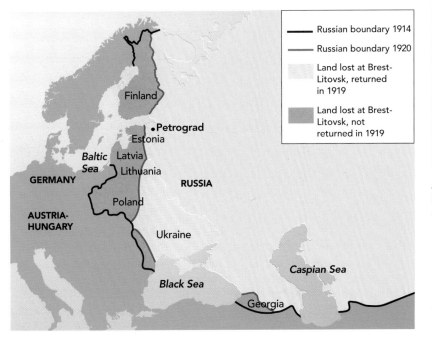

Russian boundary 1914

Russian boundary 1920

Land lost at Brest-Litovsk, returned in 1919

Land lost at Brest-Litovsk, not returned in 1919

Finland

•Petrograd
Estonia

Baltic Latvia
Sea   Lithuania

GERMANY   RUSSIA

Poland

AUSTRIA-
HUNGARY   Ukraine

Caspian Sea

Black Sea

Georgia

◀ The Treaty of Brest-Litovsk, 3 March 1918.

The price of peace

Lenin sent Trotsky, now the Minister of Foreign Affairs, to Brest-Litovsk to negotiate on Russia's behalf. Trotsky was so appalled by the German and Austrian demands that he told Lenin that they should be rejected. Lenin, however, was determined to make peace with Germany at any price. A fresh German attack in February 1918, which advanced deep into Russia, helped to confirm his belief that the government should 'yield space to buy time'. He knew Russia was on the point of civil war. It would be impossible for the government to fight the Germans and prevent its political opponents overthrowing it. On 3 March 1918 the government agreed to the Treaty of Brest-Litovsk. The treaty made Russia pay a high price for peace, in terms of land lost and money paid out in fines. Russia handed over to Germany and Austria-Hungary: Finland, Estonia, Latvia, Lithuania, Poland, Georgia and the western Ukraine. Russia also had to pay a huge fine to the Germans to compensate them for the cost of war.

The territory lost by Russia included some of its most valuable land and industry. The fertile grain lands of the Ukraine, and the rich industrial lands around the Baltic were just two of the many sacrifices made to win peace. Many people were angered by the agreement, but Lenin firmly believed that these sacrifices had saved the revolution.

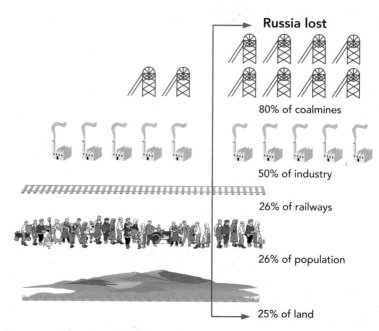

Russia lost

80% of coalmines

50% of industry

26% of railways

26% of population

25% of land

▲ Russian losses in the Treaty of Brest-Litovsk.

SUMMARY

Establishing Communist Government

1917	7-8 November	Bolsheviks seize power in Petrograd.
	November	Telegrams sent to rest of Russia.
		Sovnarkom set up.
1918	18 January	Constituent Assembly dissolved.
	February onwards	Bolshevik Party changes name.
		Reforms introduced.
	3 March	Russia left the First World War.
		Treaty of Brest-Litovsk.

BOCHKAREVA (1899–?)

Maria Bochkareva was born in the Novgorod region and began work at the age of eight. She became a prostitute at an early age, and was married by the time she was 15.

In 1914 her husband tried to kill her and she left home to join the army. She fought bravely and won many medals. In 1917 she formed the Women's Death Battalion in Petrograd and similar battalions started across Russia. Later she fled to the United States after falling out with the Bolsheviks and being sentenced to death.

Shortly after the signing of the Treaty of Brest-Litovsk, civil war broke out in Russia. Lenin's Communist government (the Reds) was opposed by a coalition of 'White' forces determined to rid Russia of communism. These White forces embraced a wide variety of views. Some of the White supporters were Monarchists who wanted the Tsar restored; others were Kerenskyists who were trying to re-establish a moderate regime such as that of the Provisional Government. Some national minority groups, such as the Cossacks in the Ukraine, supported the Whites to try to win independence from Russia. In addition to these groups were those who had personal financial reasons for opposing the Reds. Many landowners and industrialists gave their support to the Whites.

One rather unusual group of White supporters was the **Czech Legion**. In 1918 this group of 45,000 Czechoslovakian prisoners of war were being transported back home. During their journey they quarrelled with one of the local Soviets. This soon led to fighting and the Czech Legion took control of the Trans-Siberian railway, a vital link between east and west Russia. As the Reds took steps to deal with this uprising, foreign powers found the excuse they needed to intervene in the Civil War.

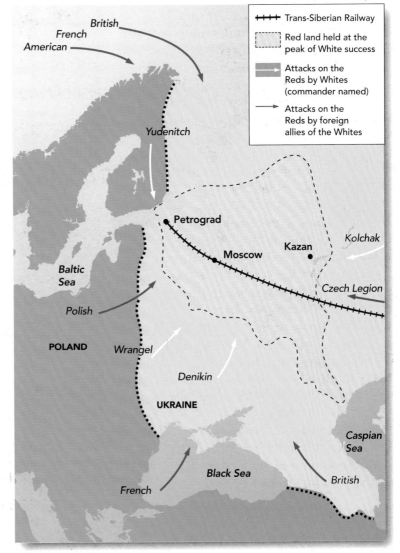

▲ **The Civil War in Russia 1918–21.**

Source B

England, America and France are waging war against Russia. They are avenging themselves on the Soviet Union for having overthrown the landowners and capitalists . . . and they are aiding and abetting the Russian landowners with money and military supplies. They, in their turn, are mounting an attack against Soviet power from Siberia, the Don and the northern Caucasus in an attempt to restore the Tsar, the landowners and the capitalists. But no! This shall never be.

▲ **A speech by Lenin in 1919.**

Foreign intervention

Russia's former allies were angry at Lenin's decision to drop out of the war. They were made even angrier by his government's announcement that it was refusing to pay all the Tsar's debts to foreign countries. They also feared that the Russian Communists would try to spark off revolutions abroad. Therefore they sent men and supplies to Russia to support the White armies. So, at one stage, the Communists were fighting not only the Whites within Russia, but the forces of fourteen different foreign countries on six separate fronts.

Yet, the Red forces were able to win the war. In the spring of 1919, White forces under General **Kolchak** invaded eastern Russia and advanced as far as Kazan. In late spring, General Deniken advanced with the White Army from the Ukraine to within 300 kilometres of Moscow. Trotsky organized a counter-attack against the White forces and drove their armies back. Kolchak was later captured and executed, Deniken resigned his command and his army was disbanded.

In the early summer of 1919, another White leader General **Yudenitch** attacked from the north and threatened Petrograd, but by the end of the year he too had been defeated.

As the White armies suffered defeats the foreign powers began to withdraw their support, but there were still problems for the Communists. The Poles launched a surprise invasion in 1920 and captured Kiev. In June 1920, a White army led by General **Wrangel** attacked from the south, hoping to link up with the invading Polish forces. But the Poles made peace and Wrangel's army was forced to withdraw.

End of the Civil War

Although some Japanese forces in the east were not defeated until 1922, the formal peace treaty with Poland (the Treaty of Riga) is seen by most historians as marking the end of the war. The Communist Red Army were victorious.

Source C

ОБМАНУТЫМЪ БРАТЬЯМЪ
(ИЗЪ БѢЛОГВАРДЕЙСКИХЪ ОКОПЪ).
Посланіе первое ДЕМЬЯНА БѢДНАГО.

▲ A Communist poster of 1918 showing the Red Army fighting the many-headed monster of the Whites. One of the heads is Tsar Nicholas.

KOLCHAK (1873–1920)

Kolchak, born Aleksandr Vasilyevich, fought in the Russo-Japanese War and commanded the Black Sea fleet during the First World War.

After the October Revolution Kolchak set up an anti-Bolshevik government at Omsk in Siberia and called himself 'Supreme Ruler of All Russia'. After his troops were defeated he resigned his office, but was captured by the Bolsheviks and shot on 7 February 1920.

1 Trotsky and the Red Army

In the months before the November revolution, the Bolsheviks had deliberately undermined the strength of the Russian army. They had encouraged soldiers to lay down their arms and desert, they had demanded that the death penalty for offences in the army be removed and had campaigned for the election of officers in the army.

In early 1918, when the Civil War broke out, the Bolsheviks paid the price for their ealier actions. They knew that a poor showing in the war would make people resent the government even more. So now, in the role of the ruling Communist party, they needed a well-disciplined and efficient army to defeat the Whites. The task of raising such an army was given to Trotsky. In March 1918 Trotsky became Chairman of the **Supreme War Council** and it was his brilliance in organization and fighting that was ultimately responsible for the Reds victory in the Civil War.

Source E

The military specialists [former officers in the Tsar's army] will be carefully watched. Any who shows signs of betraying Soviet Russia will be shot out of hand. Next to every specialist there should be a commissar [a loyal Bolshevik], one to the right, another to the left, revolver in hand.

▲ Part of Trotsky's speech to the Central Executive Committee on July 29, 1918.

▼ A Communist poster praising the three million strong Red Army.

Source D

During 1918, Trotsky introduced conscription for all men aged 18–40. These conscripts joined large numbers of people who had volunteered to fight for the cause, particularly when it became apparent that soldiers were better fed than almost anyone else in Russia. Now the Communists had an army, but most of its members were inexperienced soldiers. It was important, therefore, to get experienced officers to lead the army. Trotsky's solution was to appoint former army officers from the Tsar's army. These men found it difficult to resist Trotsky's demands as he threatened to shoot them if they refused to obey. Sometimes officers' families were taken hostage to ensure that they did their job efficiently.

Trotsky appointed party members, called **commissars**, to help run the army. For example, there was a commissar responsible for the morale of the troops, and another one for their training. Trotsky used very harsh discipline within the army, but he proved a brilliant leader and soon won the respect of his troops.

In comparison to the high morale and loyalty of the Red Army, the White forces were disunited and poorly led. They were not united by a common aim, and they were fighting over such a scattered area that it was difficult for them to co-ordinate their attacks on the Communists. They also found it difficult to win the support of the peasants, who feared that they would reverse the Communist land reforms. Perhaps most importantly, they were forced to accept foreign aid to fight the Red Army. This enabled the Communists to portray themselves as fighting for Russia against foreign invaders, thus appealing to Russian patriotism.

2 The 'Red Terror'

The Communists had many different opponents in 1917. To keep the revolution going they had to crush opposition quickly. In December 1917 Lenin set up the Extraordinary Commission for the Struggle Against Counter-Revolution, Sabotage and Speculation. This organization, which was better known as the **Cheka**, was responsible for dealing with law and order and political opposition to the Communists.

Source F

Trotsky paid a visit to the front lines. He made a speech. We were lifted by the energy which he carried wherever a critical situation arose. The situation, which had been catastrophic 24 hours earlier, had improved by his coming as though by miracle.

▲ **A Red Army soldier's description of the effect of Trotsky's leadership on troops at Gomel in 1918.**

Source G

The state police of the Tsar throttled the workers who were fighting to set up a socialist state. Our Cheka shoots landlords, capitalists and generals who are trying to restore the capitalist way of life. Do you grasp the distinction?

▲ **Trotsky replying in 1920 to the accusation that the Cheka were no different to the Tsar's Okhrana.**

In 1918 its leader, Felix Dzerhinsky, began the 'Red Terror' in which those suspected of working against the revolution were arrested, tortured and executed. In August 1918, there was a nearly successful attempt on Lenin's life. The Cheka stepped up its terror campaign. In Petrograd alone over 800 'enemies of the state' were executed. It was only after the civil war was won that the Cheka scaled down its work. By then an estimated 200,000 people had been killed and 85,000 prisoners locked away in concentration camps.

3 War communism

During the Civil War Lenin introduced a policy of war communism. The government took control of the economy. It was vital that the Red Army was supplied with the weapons and food which it needed to fight the war effectively. War communism was very effective in keeping the army supplied, but it led to widespread starvation among the peasants and workers of Russia.

Lenin set up the **Supreme Council of National Economy** to introduce war communism. Private trading was banned and profit-making was decreed to be exploitation. Factories with more than ten workers were taken over by the government and strict discipline was imposed in them. Strikes were illegal. In the countryside, peasants were encouraged to work harder still. The surplus crops they grew were taken by the government to feed the factory workers and the army. The peasants resented this. They had won the right to own their land under the Communists, but now they wanted to profit from this by selling their crops. They did not see why they should have to give surplus produce to the government. The government also abolished money charges on such services as railways and the post. This was to encourage the use of bartering instead of money. As inflation made the rouble almost worthless, many peasants did swap goods instead of using paper money.

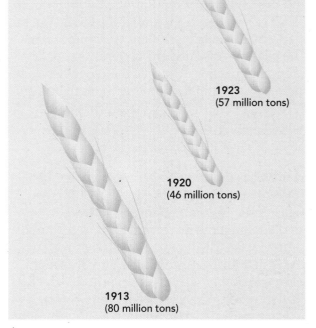

1923
(57 million tons)

1920
(46 million tons)

1913
(80 million tons)

▲ **The decline in grain production in Russia 1913–1923.**

▼ **Victims of the famine in Russia in 1921.**

Source **H**

Why was war communism abandoned?

The policy of war communism kept the army and the factory workers supplied with food. It played a vital part in winning the Civil War, but it also made the government very unpopular. The peasants resented the government policy of crop requisition. Many of them decided that there was no point in growing more than they needed – or alternatively they went to great lengths to hide food from the government forces who came to take it.

Many peasants reacted with violence when government forces arrived. By 1921 large areas of the Russian countryside were in revolt against the government. In the Tambov region 20,000 disillusioned peasants rose up and killed local communists. The peasants were put down with great severity by the Red Army and hundreds of them were executed. Peasant unrest and opposition to government policy meant food production declined. In 1921 there was a terrible famine. Millions of peasants died.

The Kronstadt mutiny

In March 1921 Lenin's government faced another blow to its authority. The sailors at the Kronstadt naval base mutinied. These sailors had been fierce supporters of the November revolution. But now they were disillusioned with the government's policies. They felt that the new government had not kept its promises. The uprising was such a serious threat to the government that Trotsky was despatched with an army of 60,000 men to deal with the sailors. In the fighting that followed thousands of the rebels were killed and many more arrested. But the victory had also cost the lives of 10,000 Red Army soldiers.

SUMMARY

The Communists win the fight for survival

▶ 1918   Trotsky creates the Red Army

           War communism keeps army supplied.

           Duma dissolved.

           Dzerhinsky and Cheka impose Red Terror.

▶ 1919   Whites defeated on battlefield.

▶ 1920   Foreign powers withdraw.

▶ 1921   War communism scrapped in face of opposition.

KOLLONTAI (1872–1952)

Alexandra Kollontai was born in St. Petersburg, daughter of an army general. She wrote radical pamphlets in support of the rights of women and factory workers, and was forced to flee Russia by the Tsar's secret police.

Whilst in exile Kollontai joined the Bolsheviks and toured the United States making speeches in favour of international socialism. She returned to Russia after the February Revolution and in October became Commissar for Public Welfare in Lenin's government. She was the only woman in this government. Her influence continued under Stalin, who made her Minister for Norway and later Ambassador to Sweden.

Source

▲ A poster issued by the Communist government in 1920, praising the role of the navy in the revolution.

New Economic Policy

The government was becoming extremely unpopular, even with people who had previously supported it. Lenin realized that a change of policy was necessary. If communism was to survive in Russia then the Communists had to adopt a less harsh economic policy. They had to win back the support of the peasants and workers – the very people for whom the revolution had been staged in November 1917. Consequently, in March 1921 Lenin introduced the New Economic Policy.

In his new policy Lenin showed that he accepted that Communist ideals could not be all be achieved immediately. He was prepared to take a step back from communism to win the support of the people of Russia. The following concessions were made in the New Economic Policy:

1 The hated practice of requisitioning grain was ended. Peasants who had enough land to grow more food than they needed (**Kulaks**) could sell any surplus for a profit. Instead of requisitioning food the government introduced a 10% tax on any profits made, which had to be paid in foodstuffs.

2 The government kept control of all large industries, but factories employing less than twenty workers were returned to private ownership and could be run on profit-making lines.

3 Private enterprise was also allowed in the retail trade. Anyone could set up a shop and sell or hire goods for a profit.

4 The practice of bartering was discouraged and instead the government encouraged people to use money once again.

The New Economic Policy was bitterly opposed by many Communists. They argued that encouraging private enterprise and profit making went against Communist principles. It was a retreat back to the evil of capitalism. Lenin, however, argued that there was simply no choice. Like the Treaty of Brest-Litovsk, the NEP was a sacrifice which had to be made if the Communists were to retain power. It was also a temporary measure. The government would regain its control of the economy when it was more secure.

Source J

We are now retreating, going back as it were, but we are doing this to retreat first and then run forward more vigorously. We retreated on this one condition alone when we introduced our New Economic Policy – so as to begin a more determined offensive after the retreat.

▲ Lenin from a speech made in 1921, explaining why the New Economic Policy was introduced.

▼ The effects of the NEP (official government figures).

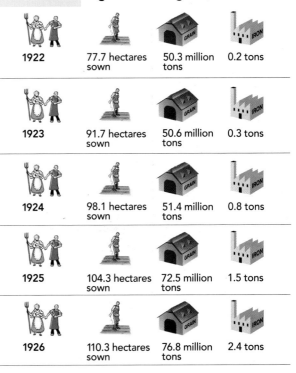

1922	77.7 hectares sown	50.3 million tons	0.2 tons
1923	91.7 hectares sown	50.6 million tons	0.3 tons
1924	98.1 hectares sown	51.4 million tons	0.8 tons
1925	104.3 hectares sown	72.5 million tons	1.5 tons
1926	110.3 hectares sown	76.8 million tons	2.4 tons

The NEP was highly successful. Peasant unrest declined sharply. Food production and industrial output gradually increased. However, the policy created future problems for Russia. Farms in the country remained small and, compared with other European countries, they were very inefficient. If Russian agriculture was to prosper, wholesale reform was necessary. Even worse, from a communist viewpoint, the NEP created a situation where some peasants, known as **Kulaks**, became wealthy by selling surplus produce. They improved their farms and began to employ poorer peasants to work for them. So Lenin's policy had not only created a new class of capitalist farmers; it had also created a situation where there would be determined resistance to any future agricultural reform – as Stalin was to discover in 1929. (See page 51).

(See page 51).

Source K

The New Economic Policy was a grudging affair. The NEP men it bred (small shop-keepers, traders, middlemen, anti-Communist to their core) improved living standards enough for the Bolsheviks to survive. In return they killed off the NEP and the NEP men as soon as they could.

▲ Brian Moynahan, in *The Russian Century*, 1994.

5.5 How did Russia become the Soviet Union?

In July 1918, the Communist government had drafted a new constitution setting up the **Russian Socialist Federal Soviet Republic**. It reflected the importance of the Soviets in the running of the country. In theory the supreme authority in the country was the All-Russian Congress of Soviets which would elect an executive committee of 200 members. This committee would elect the Council of People's Commissars to run the country. In practice the decisions were made by Lenin, who paid only lip service to the constitution.

In 1924 Russia formally changed its name to the **Union Of Soviet Socialist Republics**, or the Soviet Union as it was to be known in the west. The country was set up as a union of four republics, Russia, the Ukraine, Byelorussia and the Caucasus. Each had control over local matters, such as education. Control of matters such as foreign policy and the armed forces remained in the hands of the national government, which, from 1918, was based in Moscow.

Source L

► A Russian poster from October 1918, celebrating one year of Bolshevik government. Through the window can be seen the dream of a productive communist Russia. The worker and peasant are standing on symbols representing the evils of the past.

CHKHEIDZEI (1864–1926)

Nikolai Chkheidzei was a Social Democrat who played an important part in the first Duma of 1907 and became President of the Petrograd Soviet. He disapproved of the Bolshevik takeover and, after failing to establish an independent republic in his native Georgia, he fled to France in 1921. Trotsky wrote to Nikolai in 1913 and criticized Lenin in his letter. Stalin later used this letter to discredit Trotsky.

The death of Lenin

In the spring of 1922 Lenin suffered a massive stroke, followed by further strokes in December 1922 and March 1923. Finally, in January 1924, he died. His body lay in state for a week after his death while thousands of mourners queued in the freezing weather to pay their last respects. After the funeral his body was not buried or cremated, but instead was embalmed and put on show in a specially built mausoleum in Moscow. Since then millions of visitors from around the world have visited his tomb. As a further honour, Petrograd, the city where the November revolution had taken place, was renamed Leningrad. But although Lenin is seen as a hero by Russian people, and many historians, there are those who believe that he does not deserve the adulation he has received.

Source 1

Of all the tyrannies in history, the Bolshevik tyranny is the worst, the most destructive, the most degrading. The atrocities committed under Lenin and Trotsky are incomparably more hideous and more numerous than anything for which the Kaiser is responsible.

▲ Speech made by Winston Churchill, British Secretary for War and Air, in 1919.

Source 3

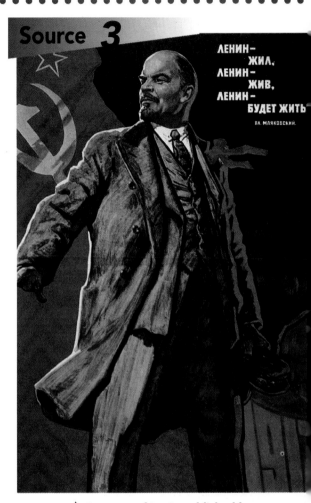

▲ A poster of Lenin published by the Soviet government in 1967.

Source 2

▲ A picture painted during Lenin's lifetime showing him meeting leaders of people of eastern Russia. In the background are Trostky and Dzerhinsky.

Source 4

It seemed as if one dictatorship, that of the Tsars, had simply been replaced by another, that of Lenin and his Communist Party. A one-party state, a secret police and a 'party' army did not look like much of a change to most Russians.

▲ A modern historian commenting on the situation in Russia in 1918.

Source 5

ТОВ. Ленин ОЧИЩАЕТ
землю от нечисти.

▲ A poster issued by Lenin's government showing him sweeping away the royal family, aristocrats, church and capitalists. It is entitled *'Lenin Cleans the Earth of Evil Spirits'*.

► Extract from an article by Lenin's widow, Krupskaya, in the party newspaper, *Pravda*, shortly after his death.

Source 7

Do not build memorials to him, name palaces after him, do not hold magnificent celebrations in his memory. All of this meant so little to him.

Source 8

► Extract from the British newspaper, the *Morning Post*, in 1924.

Lenin was one of the most sinister and sombre figures that ever darkened the human stage. This evil man was the founder and mainstay of Bolshevism. It is a great mistake to look upon him as a moderate. He was a revolutionary whose thirst for power could never be quenched.

Source 6

Comrade Lenin possessed an immense personal magnetism; when he began to speak complete silence fell over the hall; all eyes were upon him. Comrade Lenin would glance at the audience as if hypnotizing it. I watched the big crowd and did not see a single person move or cough during those three hours. Comrade Lenin is the greatest speaker I have ever heard.

▲ Katayama, organizer of the Japanese Communist Party, describes a speech by Lenin in 1921.

Was Lenin a 'Red Tyrant'?

To the Soviet Union of the mid-twentieth century Lenin was a great hero. He had helped to organize the Bolshevik Party, had returned to Russia in 1917 to lead the Revolution, and had become the first Communist ruler of the new Soviet Union. Whilst he was in power the Communists had defeated their enemies and set the country on the road to Communist utopia. This image is seen quite clearly in Sources 2 and 3.

Yet to Russia's political opponents such as Winston Churchill in Source 1, Lenin offered no more than a substitute for the autocratic rule of the Tsar. The Russian people still had to endure hardship and lack of political freedom.

Tyrants force their subjects to obey them. Did Lenin use force, or were the Russian people prepared to suffer in the cause of a fairer social system? The eight sources in these pages give a variety of opinions to help you decide what you think.

CHAPTER 6

STALIN AND THE MODERNIZATION OF THE SOVIET UNION

When Lenin died in 1924 there was a power struggle to see who should succeed him. By 1929 Stalin had emerged as Lenin's successor. Stalin was determined that the Soviet Union should be modernized to make it strong enough to resist the attack from the west which he was sure would come. Despite fierce opposition, he implemented a policy of **collectivization** in agriculture and a series of **Five Year Plans** to bring Soviet industry up to date. By 1941, when **Nazi Germany** invaded the Soviet Union, Stalin's country was strong enough to resist the invasion, though only after terrible sacrifices by the Soviet people. However, Stalin was determined to wipe out any opposition. Millions of Soviet citizens died in his **'purges'**. It was small wonder that the cruelty of Stalin's leadership was attacked by his successor, Khrushchev, in 1956.

Source A

▲ A painting of Lenin speaking with Stalin sitting by his side. The painting, entitled *Comrade-in-arms at the First All-Russian Congress of Soviets, June 1917* was painted after Lenin's death.

6.1 Why did Stalin take over after Lenin's death?

When Lenin died in 1924 it was widely believed Trotsky would take over. As commander of the Red Army, Trotsky had played an important part in winning the Civil War. He was also a brilliant speaker who was well known for the passion with which he put across his views in party meetings. But, while Trotsky was very able, he was also arrogant and prone to flashes of temper. This made him unpopular with the other senior members of the Communist Party. Lenin himself had warned his colleagues that Trotsky displayed 'excessive self-assurance'.

Immediately after Lenin's death, there was a period when the seven members of the **Politburo** (the ruling body of the Communist Party) ran the country between them. They spent most of their time locked in a struggle for the leadership. Two serious contenders emerged – Trotsky and Stalin.

MEMBERS OF THE POLITBURO IN 1924

Trotsky:	Commissar for War
Stalin:	Secretary of the Communist Party
Kamenev:	Chairman of the Politburo
Rykov:	Chairman of Sovnarkom
Zinoviev:	Chairman of Comintern*
Bukharin:	responsible for propaganda
Tomsky:	responsible for trade union affairs

An organization set up in 1919 to help Communists in other countries

Stalin was well placed to take over. He was Secretary of the Party and so controlled appointments to posts in the Party. Trotsky had spent a long period touring Russia, fighting the Civil War, whereas Stalin had been making allies within the Party and trying to establish a good relationship with Lenin, though there is little doubt that Lenin did not actually like Stalin. In 1923 Lenin had written to Stalin telling him to apologize for being rude to Lenin's wife. The postscript to Lenin's *Testament* made it clear that he considered Stalin unsuitable as a leader.

But when Lenin died in January 1924 the *Testament* had not been made public. Stalin made numerous speeches in praise of the dead hero and played a prominent part in the funeral ceremony. Trotsky was not at the funeral. He was in southern Russia recovering from malaria when Lenin died. He later claimed that he phoned Moscow to find out when the funeral was, and that Stalin gave him the wrong date, saying there was not time for Trotsky to return. Since Trotsky and Stalin became bitter rivals, it is easy to believe this story, but it is equally possible that Trotsky fabricated it to show Stalin in a poor light.

Source C

Comrade Stalin, having become Secretary has unlimited authority concentrated in his hands and I am not sure whether he will be capable of using that authority with sufficient caution. Comrade Trotsky, on the other hand, is distinguished not only by his outstanding ability. He is perhaps the most capable man in the present Committee – but he has displayed excessive self-assurance . . .

▲ Lenin's views on Stalin and Trotsky, as set out in a letter he wrote to the Party just before his death. The letter has become known as his *Testament*.

Source B

Stalin is too rude, and this fault is intolerable in the office of Secretary. Therefore I propose to comrades that they find a way of removing Stalin from his post and appointing another man who is more patient, more loyal, more polite and is considerate to his comrades.

▲ A postscript to Lenin's *Testament*, written ten days after the main letter.

Source D

▶ Lenin making a speech in 1920. The two men standing beside the rostrum are Trotsky and Kamenev. When this photograph was published again after Stalin came to power, Trotsky and Kamenev's pictures had been removed from it.

Stalin vs. Trotsky

One of the major differences between Trotsky and Stalin concerned their attitude towards the spread of communism. Trotsky believed in theory of 'permanent revolution'. He felt that communism could not survive in the Soviet Union unless the communist revolution spread to other countries. Trotsky argued that it was the duty of the Soviet Union to help revolutionary groups in other countries. Stalin, however, believed in 'socialism in one country'. He felt that the Soviet Union should concentrate on establishing communism at home, making itself a modern and powerful country, rather than trying to bring about world-wide revolution.

Stalin was supported by Kamenev and Zinoviev. These three members of the Politburo made sure that Trotsky did not succeed Lenin as party leader. Equally importantly, Zinoviev and Kamenev persuaded the other members of the Politburo not to expel Stalin from his post as Secretary and not to embarrass him by publishing Lenin's *Testament*.

Trotsky into exile

From 1924 Trotsky was gradually relieved of his positions in the Party until, in 1929, he was exiled from the Soviet Union. Stalin no longer needed Zinoviev and Kamenev, who both wanted to end the NEP, which Stalin supported. Stalin now had enough power in the Politburo to have them expelled.

By the end of 1929 Stalin had also forced Bukharin, Rykov and Tomsky to resign from the Politburo, which was now packed with his own supporters. The battle for the leadership was over. Stalin was now firmly in control in the Soviet Union.

Source E

As for Trotsky, he was a coward during the time of the Brest-Litovsk negotiations and the greatest victories in the Civil War were won in spite of him. Neither in the party, nor in the uprising, did Trotsky play any special role, nor could he do so in the October days he was relatively new in our party.

▲ Part of a speech made by Stalin in 1924.

THE DOWNFALL OF TROTSKY

► 1925 Resigned as Commissar for War.
► 1926 Expelled from Politburo.
► 1927 Expelled from Communist Party.
► 1928 Deported to Soviet Central Asia.
► 1929 Exiled from the Soviet Union.

ZINOVIEV (1883–1936)

Zinoviev was born Grigory Yevseyevich in Yelizavotgrad (now Kirovgrad). He joined the Social Democrats in 1901 and became a firm supporter of Lenin. Zinoviev was active in the 1905 Revolution and was forced into exile from 1905–17. In 1917 he returned to Russia. He was Chairman of the Leningrad Soviet, a member of the Politburo, and from 1919–26 was Chairman of the Executive Committee of the Comintern.

After Lenin's death Zinoviev was considered to be a serious rival by Stalin, who had him expelled from the party in 1927 as a supporter of Trotsky. He was readmitted but later expelled again. In 1935 he was sentenced to 10 years' imprisonment for 'moral complicity' in Kirov's murder. He was retried in 1936 and executed.

When Stalin came to power, the Soviet Union's economy could not compete with those of the great western powers such as Britain, Germany and the United States. Stalin feared that communism would not survive unless the Soviet Union could compete with other nations. He began a policy of industrial development designed to transform the Soviet Union from an agricultural country into a major industrial power in just a few years. Stalin used the State Planning Commission (**Gosplan**), set up by Lenin in 1921, to run the economic development of the Soviet Union. In 1928 Gosplan came up with its first Five Year Plan. It set targets for production across a wide range of industry, power supply and transport. The targets set were often unrealistic, but workers across the Soviet Union were encouraged by the use of propaganda and rewards to meet their individual targets. Those who failed were likely to face punishments such as fines, or even losing their jobs.

Source F

The tempo must not be reduced. To slacken the pace would mean to lag behind, and those who lag behind are beaten. We do not want to be beaten. We are fifty to a hundred years behind the advanced countries. We must make good this lag in ten years. Either we do it, or they crush us.

▲ **Extract from a speech by Stalin in 1931.**

Peasants into workers

To encourage workers to produce more the government had to change working practices. Many of the factory workers in the Soviet Union in the early 1930s had previously been peasants, used to working at their own speed. Such a system was not likely to bring about increased production. So the government laid down strict rules and regulations for workers. Absenteeism was not permitted and workers who took time off were likely to lose their jobs and be evicted from their homes. They also lost their ration cards which made it very difficult for them to buy food.

Under the Five Year Plan good workers who kept up their production rates received high salaries, but for many people the targets were just too high. In 1929 the government said that factories would open seven days a week and workers would take their days off by rota.

Many workers began to find factory work too demanding and left to work somewhere else. In 1932 the government introduced internal passports. Workers could not move from one town to another without permission.

▲ **'We Smite the Lazy Workers'. A Soviet poster from 1931.**

The Stakhanovite movement

Some more enthusiastic and younger workers joined **shock brigades** which strove to beat previous production levels and show other workers just what could be achieved. These workers received special rates of pay and better housing. Some of the very best workers were awarded medals for service to the state. These were called Stakhanovites after Alexei Stakhanov, the Georgian miner. In 1934 Stakhanov organized his fellow workers to cut 102 tons of coal in a single shift. The target for the shift was just seven tons. Stakhanov became a national hero. His picture appeared on the front of newspapers and he was invited to meet other workers to explain his methods. However, the Stakhanovites were hated by their fellow workers and in 1936 the British consul in Leningrad reported that 'people are sick of Stakhanov'. As harsh targets and constant propaganda began to make workers resentful, so the Stakhanovites movement was no longer promoted by the government.

▲ The Great Man: Alexei Stakhanov explaining his methods to fellow workers.

Labour camps

One government policy which was kept very quiet was the use of **labour camps**. Huge camps were set up to house opponents of Stalin's regime. These ranged from peasants who opposed the policy of **collectivization** (see page 52) to intellectuals and writers who criticized the government. Stalin claimed these people would be cleansed of their anti-social views by undertaking useful employment. They worked as slave labour building roads, bridges and canals. Their most famous achievement was to drive a canal 500 kilometres from the White Sea to the Baltic Sea.

The camps were supervised by a special department of the secret police called Gulag. We know about them mainly through the works of the Soviet **dissident**, Alexander Solzhenitsyn, who spent many years in them. He talks about people freezing to death in temperatures so low that the mercury in the thermometers froze. Living conditions were appalling and food supplies were inadequate. In 1928 there were around 30,000 prisoners in the labour camps. By 1938 it was around 7,000,000. In the years 1937–8, about 7,000,000 prisoners were sent to labour camps and during that time about 2,000,000 of them died. No one knows the exact figures of deaths in the labour camps, but during Stalin's rule it may well have been as high as 12,000,000.

At the end of the workday there were corpses left on the work site. At night the sledges went out and got them. In the summer bones remained from corpses which had not been removed in time, and together with the shingle they got into the concrete mixer. In this way they got into the concrete on the last lock at the city of Belomorsk and will be preserved for ever.

▲ Extract from a book by Russian dissident writer Alexander Solzhenitsyn, *The Gulag Archipelago*, 1974.

More Five Year Plans

In 1929 Stalin decided that the Five Year Plan should reach its targets in just four years. So in 1932 a second Five Year Plan was drawn up to run until 1938. This plan concentrated on producing tractors for the new collectivized farms (see page 52) and on machinery and tools for the factories. There were also to be improvements in all types of transport. In reality, much of the production was centred around war goods as Stalin became increasingly concerned that his country might go to war with Nazi Germany.

The third Five Year Plan was launched in 1938. This plan concentrated on the production of household goods and luxuries such as radios and bicycles, in an attempt to provide Soviet citizens with some of the consumer goods common in industrialized countries. The quality of goods needed to improve, too; almost 40% of production in the first two plans had to be scrapped as faulty. This plan was interrupted in 1941 when Nazi Germany invaded the Soviet Union. A fourth Five Year Plan was introduced in 1946 to rebuild the country after the war and proved to be a great success.

The Five Year Plans had a dramatic effect on the Soviet Union. In just ten years it became the second largest industrial power in the world. Huge new steel plants, hydro-electric power stations, railways and canals were all built. Vast numbers of factories in hundreds of new towns poured out manufactured goods. A major symbol of this growth was the new town of Magnitogorsk. Between 1928 and 1932 it was transformed from a tiny village in the Ural mountains to a thriving industrial city with more than a quarter of a million citizens. Stalin had brought about the industrialization of the Soviet Union at an enormous cost, but his aim to make his country strong enough to withstand an attack from Nazi Germany had been achieved, as events from 1941–5 were to show.

JOE SCOTT

Joe Scott was an American who was inspired by the ideals of the Russian Revolution. A graduate of Wisconsin University, he trained as a welder and went to Russia as a volunteer at the gigantic iron and steel works being set up at Magnitogorsk in 1929. He wanted to join 'a society that was at least one step in front of America,' he said. His diary gives the point of view of a sympathetic outsider. He was stunned by the harsh conditions, under which 'men froze, hungered and suffered, and by the spirit with which the work went on with a complete disregard for individual and personal considerations'.

Source J

	1928	1932	1937
Coal	36	66	139
Iron	3	6	15
Steel	4	6	18
Oil	12	23	29

▲ The growth of Soviet industry 1928–37. Figures given are output in million tons.

Source K

In early April it was still bitter cold, everything was frozen. By May the city was swimming in mud. Bubonic plague had broken out not far from Magnitogorsk. The resistance of the population was very low because of undernourishment and consistent overwork. Sanitary conditions were appalling. By the middle of May the heat was intolerable.

▲ Description of the working conditions in Magnitogorsk by J. Scott, an American engineer.

SUMMARY

The Modernization of Soviet Industry

▶ 1921 Gosplan set up.

▶ 1928 First Five Year Plan.

    Strict targets set.

    Control of working practices.

    Labour camps.

▶ 1932 Second Five Year Plan.

▶ 1938 Third Five Year Plan.

▶ 1946 Fourth Five Year Plan.

Stalin's determination that Soviet industry should develop rapidly relied on the workers in the city being well-fed. But the NEP introduced by Lenin was failing to produce enough food. One reason was that Soviet farming techniques were inefficient.

By 1927 Stalin had decided that the Soviet Union's farming problems needed solving quickly. The vast majority of Soviet citizens were still peasants who owned tiny pieces of land which they cultivated using the old **strip farming** system. Many of them were too poor to afford modern equipment. Even in the late 1920s most peasants used a horse-drawn wooden plough not a tractor. But Stalin knew that the NEP had also created another problem. It had produced a class of richer peasants, the Kulaks, who were reluctant to sell their produce to the government at the low price that was on offer. They preferred to store it, hoping the price would rise. If changes were to be brought about in farming, something would have to be done about the Kulaks.

Source M

▲ A group of Soviet peasants carrying a banner with the inscription 'We demand collectivization and the wiping out of all Kulaks'.

Source L

Don't you see, isn't it time you stopped thinking each one for himself and for his piggish hide? ... You Kulaks, of course, will never become reconciled to a new order. You love to fatten on other people's blood. But we know how to deal with you. We'll wipe you off the face of the earth.

▲ A government official addressing a group of villagers on why they should join a collective farm.

Source N

Look at the Kulak farms: their barns and sheds are crammed with grain. They are waiting for prices to rise. So long as there are Kulaks there will be sabotage of grain procurements. The effect will be that our towns and industrial centres, as well as our Red Army, will be in grave difficulties; they will be poorly supplied and will be threatened with hunger; we cannot allow that.

We must break the resistance of this class and deprive it of its existence. This is necessary in order to be able to dispense with importing grain and to save foreign currency for the development of industry.

▲ Extracts from speeches made about collectivization by Stalin in 1928 and 1929.

Source O

КУЛАКИ САМЫЕ ЗВЕРСКИЕ,
САМЫЕ ГРУБЫЕ, САМЫЕ ДИ-
КИЕ, ЭКСПЛООАТАТОРЫ, НЕ
РАЗ ВОССТАНАВЛИВАВШИЕ
В ИСТОРИИ ДРУГИХ СТРАН
ВЛАСТЬ ПОМЕЩИКОВ, ЦАРЕЙ,
ПОПОВ И КАПИТАЛИСТОВ.
ЛЕНИН.

ДОЛОЙ КУЛАКА ИЗ КОЛХОЗА

▲ A government poster of a Kulak.

Source P

Millions of peasants, rather than give up their livestock to the collectives without compensation, preferred to kill their cows, sheep, and chickens. For a brief period Russia ate more meat than it had eaten in decades. Then it went on a vegetarian diet.

▲ An American newspaper reporter commenting on what he saw in the Soviet Union in 1930.

Getting rid of the Kulaks

When the revolution came in 1917 the Communists had hoped to introduce common land ownership, where all the peasants worked for the common good of the Soviet people. The Kulaks were an embarrassment to the government because they were a class of 'agricultural capitalists'. Communism did not allow for individual profit making. Stalin decided that the Kulaks would have to go. By 1928 Stalin was ready to act. He could see the very real possibility of starvation in the cities. He sent the army into the countryside to enforce the policy of 'grain procurement' (in reality this meant buying up grain at very low prices). He introduced rationing in the cities. Even so, his measures did not solve the problem.

Collectivization

Then, in 1929, Stalin announced that Soviet farming was to be **collectivized**. Peasants were to pool their fields and equipment to set up **collective farms** (**Kolkhozs**), which would be big enough to afford mechanized equipment and would be much more efficient than the tiny farms. Motor Tractor Stations would be set up to supply the collective farms with tractors.

As compensation, peasants could keep small plots of land around their cottages. Peasants would be paid a wage for working and their produce would be sold to the government at a low price. The practice of selling crops on the open market for a profit would cease. Stalin was aware that collectivization would be extremely unpopular with the Kulaks. He decided that if they would not volunteer to join collective farms, he would wipe them out as a class. In effect, this is what he did.

Arrests and deportations

Officials were sent into the countryside to persuade the peasant farmers to accept collectivization. Not surprisingly many of them refused to give up their land and livestock to the collective farms. The government had to use force. The Red Army and the state police arrested and deported millions of peasants. Most of the estimated 5,000,000 Kulaks were exiled to remote parts of the country or sent to labour camps, where many of them died.

Food shortages and starvation

But the peasants did not give up without a fight. Many of them slaughtered their animals and destroyed their crops rather than hand them over to the collectives. The result was that agricultural production declined dramatically (see Source Q) and in 1932–3 the Soviet Union suffered a terrible famine. There was widespread starvation.

Food shortages were so bad that cannibalism was reported. It is hard to quantify the number of peasants who died; some historians have put the figure as high as 10,000,000. Although his people were starving Stalin thought it more important to export grain to other countries to raise the money to buy raw materials and machinery for Soviet industry.

Yet, despite the terrible problems of the early 1930s, collectivization was ultimately a success, although it became a success at enormous cost to the Soviet people. Stalin used the might of the government to break the Kulaks and force the peasants into the Kolkhozs. By 1937, over ninety per cent of peasant farms had been collectivized and the Kulaks had been destroyed.

From 1933 Soviet agricultural production improved; by 1937 output was significantly higher. More and more peasants had tractors. They were also benefitting from government schemes to improve literacy on the farms. Stalin had brought about a revolution in agriculture in much the same way that he had revolutionized industry.

Source R

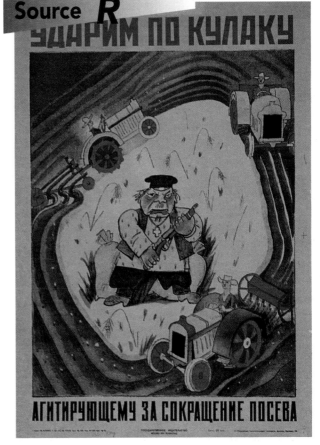

▲
A government poster showing an anti-social Kulak guarding his plot while tractors cultivate collective land all around him.

SOLZHENITSYN (1918–)

Alexander Solzhenitsyn graduated from Rostov University in Maths and Physics in 1941. He served in the Red Army, but was arrested in 1945 for making critical comments about Stalin.

Following his imprisonment, Solzhenitsyn wrote *One Day in the Life of Ivan Denisovich*, published in 1962, making Solzhenitsyn a national hero. In 1970 he won the Nobel Prize for literature, but was not allowed to collect it. Finally, he was expelled from Russia after slating it in a new novel, *Gulag Archipelago*.

Source Q

Number of livestock in the Soviet Union 1928–33
(Figures are in millions).

	1928	1929	1930	1931	1932	1933
Cattle	71	67	53	48	41	38
Pigs	26	20	14	14	12	12
Sheep and goats	147	147	109	78	52	50

6.4 How did Stalin deal with opposition in the Soviet Union?

Although by 1928 Stalin was in total command of the Soviet Union, his policies of collectivization and industrialization had made him many opponents. During the 1930s, Stalin became increasingly concerned that his enemies were plotting to overthrow him. He took steps to deal with people who had opposed him in the past or who he suspected might do so in the future. These were 'the purges' in which Stalin eliminated those he called 'enemies of the state'. Over 40,000,000 people were arrested in the years 1936–53. Some 24,000,000 of them were executed or died in labour camps.

Many of those who were 'purged' were loyal Communists with years of service to the Party. Often they simply could not believe what was happening to them and were convinced that some terrible mistake had been made. The majority of Stalin's victims were ordinary people such as teachers and factory workers who had for some, usually unknown, reason fallen out with the authorities. Few of the victims actually wanted to overthrow communism or replace Stalin with the exiled Trotsky.

Various explanations have been put forward for Stalin's purges. Some historians believe that he suffered from a persecution complex or that once the campaign started it was difficult to stop it snowballing. Others have concluded that mass arrests and deportations to labour camps were the only way that Stalin could find a labour force to work in the more inhospitable parts of the Soviet Union.

Source T

Among the Trotskyites and Zinovievites fascism found faithful servants who were ready to work for the defeat of the Soviet Union in order to restore capitalism. Trotsky, Zinoviev and Kamenev have been in conspiracy against Lenin, the Party and the Soviet state ever since the October revolution.

▲ Stalin writing in his *History of the Communist Party of the Soviet Union* in 1939.

Source U

Many genuine old Bolsheviks who were arrested at this time simply refused to believe that this had happened with his [Stalin's] knowledge, still less on his personal instructions. They wrote to him. Some of them, after being tortured, inscribed 'Long live Stalin' in blood on the walls of their prison.

▲ The poet Yevtushenko remembers the time of the purges in his autobiography.

Source S

◄ A satirical cartoon published in Paris in the 1930s. Its caption says *'Visit the Pyramids of the USSR'*.

▲ A cartoon from an American newspaper in the 1930s.

Show trials and purges

The purges began after the assassination of Sergei Kirov in December 1934. Kirov was a popular leading Communist and member of the Politburo. The circumstances surrounding his death are very suspicious. Stalin's state police seem to have been aware that the assassin, Nikolayev, intended to murder Kirov. Some Soviet historians believe that Stalin let Kirov die. The assassination removed a potential rival and provided Stalin with an excuse to take measures to deal with supposed opposition. This view helps explain why Nikoleyev was tried in secret and promptly executed.

Stalin now accused two prominent Communists, Kamenev and Zinoviev, of having plotted against him and of being involved in Kirov's assassination. They were arrested and given long prison sentences. Then, in 1936, Kamenev, Zinoviev and fourteen others were charged with conspiring with Trotsky to overthrow the government. They all confessed to their crimes and were executed. Their trial was the first of the **show trials** in which leading Communists confessed to crimes involving trying to overthrow the government.

Most of these crimes involved supporting Trotsky in his attempt to overthrow Stalin. Few, if any, of these people were guilty of the crimes to which they confessed. Their confession often followed periods of torture, or a false promise that they would not be executed if they confessed. Others were told that their families would be punished if they did not make a public confession. In addition to those who were tried in public, thousands of other party members were executed or sent to labour camps.

Source W

The judge asked 'Don't you know that Kirov was killed in Leningrad?'
I replied 'Yes, but it wasn't I who killed him, it was someone called Nikolayev. And I've never been to Leningrad in my life.'
The judge snapped 'Are you a lawyer or something? All right you've never been to Leningrad, but Kirov was killed by people who shared your ideas, so you share the moral and criminal responsibility'.

The officials then 'withdrew for consultation', but were back within two minutes. The judge had a large sheet of paper in his hand covered with a closely typed and neatly laid out text. It must have taken twenty minutes to type. He announced the verdict. 'Ten years maximum isolation in prison'.

▲ Eugenia Ginzburg, a university lecturer, describes her seven minute trial for alleged involvement in the murder of Kirov. As a result of the trial she served eighteen years in a labour camp.

Source X

I should like to repeat that I am fully and utterly guilty. I am guilty of having been the organizer, second only to Trotsky, of that group whose chosen task was the killing of Stalin.

▲ Part of the confession made by Zinoviev in his trial.

Lenin's General Staff of 1917

STALIN, THE EXECUTIONER, ALONE REMAINS

RYKOV Shot	BUKHARIN Shot	SVERDLOV Dead	STALIN Survivor	ZINOVIEV Shot	KAMENEV Shot	TROTSKY In Exile	LENIN Dead
KOLLONTAI Missing?	URITSKY Dead	KRESTINSKY Shot	SMILGA Shot	NOGIN Dead	DZERZHINSKY Dead	BUBNOV Disappeared	SOKOLNIKOV In Prison
LOMOV ?	SHOMYAN Dead	BERZIN ?	MURANOV Disappeared	ARTEM Dead	STASSOVA Disappeared	MILIUTIN Missing	JOFFE Suicide

The Central Committee of The Bolshevik Party in 1917

◄ A picture published in an American newspaper by followers of Trotsky in the 1930s.

Stalin's attack on leading party members was just the tip of the iceberg. The purges spread to all walks of Soviet society. In 1937, Marshal Tuchachevsky, the commander-in-chief of the Red Army, and seven other generals were arrested. They were shot as spies without ever being brought to trial. By 1938 some 25,000 army officers had been purged. Millions of ordinary citizens were also arrested by the secret police, often after being reported by neighbours with a grudge against them.

By 1938, when Stalin relaxed his purges, there can have been few people with enough courage to speak out against him, let alone organize resistance to him. Stalin had stamped out potential opposition, but at the same time he had undermined much of his earlier work of building up industry and the army. Able scientists, politicians, administrators, engineers and (perhaps most significantly) about two-thirds of the Red Army's officers had been executed or sent to labour camps. The supposed architect of opposition to Stalin, Trotsky, was murdered by one of Stalin's agents in Mexico in 1940.

SUMMARY

Stalin's Purges – 1934

- ▶ Kirov assassinated.
- ▶ Stalin begins purges of 'enemies of the state'.
- ▶ Estimated 40,000,000 people arrested.
- ▶ Victims came from all walks of life.
- ▶ Many victims confess in show trials.
- ▶ Trotsky murdered in 1940.

NADEZHDA ALLILUYEVA (1901–32)

Nadezhda Alliluyeva was a Bolshevik who became Stalin's second wife in 1918. She did not have the same commitment to the party as Stalin, and in 1921 was expelled as a 'non-activist', although Stalin had her reinstated. She studied at the Industrial Academy, where she met Nikita Khrushchev and introduced him to her husband.

Nadezhda was extremely concerned about the social costs of her husband's policies and in 1932 made a speech about the miseries being suffered by the people. The next day she committed suicide. Her death was a great embarrassment to Stalin.

CHAPTER 7

THE IMPACT OF THE SECOND WORLD WAR

Ever since Hitler came to power in January 1933 the Soviet Union had feared an invasion by Germany. Hitler made no secret of his contempt for the Slav people who lived in parts of the Soviet Union and referred to them as *Untermenschen* (sub-humans). He wanted to conquer the Soviet Union and take control of its valuable oilfields and farmlands. German settlers could control the country with the Soviet people working as slave labourers. In 1939, Germany and the Soviet Union signed the Nazi-Soviet Pact. It appeared that the two enemies, Hitler and Stalin had become friends. Yet in reality the Pact was no more than a 'marriage of convenience'. Hitler wanted to invade Poland without opposition from the Soviets. Stalin wanted to remain on good terms with Hitler so that he had time to build up Soviet forces before the inevitable German attack was launched.

Source A

THE SCUM OF THE EARTH, I BELIEVE ?

THE BLOODY ASSASSIN OF THE WORKERS, I PRESUME ?

▲ A British cartoon about the Nazi-Soviet Pact, published in 1939.

▼ The German invasion of the Soviet Union.

Countries occupied by or allied with Germany	▲▲▲▲▲ German start line, 1941
Soviet Union	▲▲▲▲▲ Furthest extent of German line
Neutral countries	

7.1 Operation Barbarossa starts

That attack came in June 1941, when the Germans launched **Operation Barbarossa**. Three powerful armies drove deep into the Soviet Union at a rate of 70 kilometres a day. The German **Luftwaffe** (airforce) destroyed most of the Soviet planes on the ground.

By the end of October 1941, German troops had destroyed 20,000 Soviet tanks and taken 2,000,000 prisoners. In the south they had captured Kiev and further north were in sight of both Leningrad and Moscow.

Defeated by winter

Yet the German attack ultimately proved unsuccessful. In November 1941 temperatures began to drop as the Soviet winter set in. The Germans had expected to defeat the Soviets before the worst of the winter took hold, but this had not happened. Now they found themselves unprepared for the ferocity of the winter weather. Temperatures reached -35°C and soon more than 1,000,000 of the original 3,000,000 German soldiers were suffering from frostbite. Oil froze in the tanks and machine guns jammed. On 6 December, General Zhukov launched a counter attack on German troops advancing on Moscow. The Germans were forced to abandon their advance.

The German position was also made worse by the Soviet scorched earth policy. As the German advance reached individual villages, so the villagers deliberately destroyed anything of value to the Germans which could not be carried away. Consequently, the German armies found themselves deep in Soviet territory and running very short of supplies. Yet when the spring came Hitler ordered his troops to advance once more. The main attacks were concentrated on Leningrad in the north and Stalingrad in the south. Leningrad had been under siege since September 1941. Heroic resistance prevented the city from falling into German hands in 1942, but the siege continued for 900 days until January 1944, when the Germans were finally defeated. The civilian population, which had been reduced to eating cats, dogs, worms and even wallpaper glue, had suffered terrible hardships in which almost 1,000,000 of them had died.

The fight for Stalingrad

In the south, two German armies advanced on Stalingrad in September 1942. Hitler was determined that the city was to be taken at all costs. But Soviet resistance was equally determined. As the Germans attacked the city they were forced to fight to gain control of every house in every street. In November 1942 Soviet forces launched a counter-attack which surrounded the Germans and made their defeat inevitable. Hitler told the German commander, Von Paulus, that under no circumstances must he surrender. Von Paulus held out until January 1943, when he felt that he could not go on fighting. He surrendered and 100,000 German soldiers were taken prisoner. A further 150,000 had died trying to capture the city.

Source B

The enemy must not be left a single engine or single railway truck. Collective farmers must drive off all their cattle and turn their grain over to the safe-keeping of the State authorities. All valuable property that cannot be withdrawn must be destroyed without fail. In areas occupied by the enemy, sabotage groups must be organized to combat enemy units. In these regions conditions must be made unbearable for the enemy.

▲ Part of a radio speech made by Stalin on 3 July 1941.

Source C

Soviet soldiers acquired tremendous experience in hand-to-hand fighting. They knew every drainpipe, every manhole, every shell-hole and crater. Among piles of rubble, which no tanks could penetrate, he would turn on his machine gun the moment he saw a German within firing distance. Seldom anything short of a direct hit could knock him out.

▲ The Soviet general, Talensky, describes the heroism of Soviet troops defending Stalingrad in 1942.

The battle for Stalingrad was a turning point in the war in the Soviet Union. Hitler launched another offensive in the summer of 1943, but it was driven back after the Soviets won a massive tank battle at Kursk in July. Hitler had anticipated a glorious victory in the Soviet Union. His invasion became a desperate retreat to Germany. By mid-1944 Soviet forces had driven the Germans out of the Soviet Union. In April 1945 they entered the German capital, Berlin.

Victory at a great cost

Soviet victory in the war was a great boost to Stalin. He had been an effective war-time leader, rapidly mobilizing his country's resources against the invading enemy. The government had organized a huge evacuation of factories and raw materials to the safety of the Urals in 1941, and it was from here that the equipment to win the war was produced. But the war had been won at enormous cost. Huge areas of farmland and thousands of factories had been destroyed. More than 20,000,000 Soviet citizens were killed in the war. 70,000 villages and nearly 2,000 towns and cities were destroyed. More Soviet people died defending Stalingrad than the United States lost in the whole war. The occupying German forces showed the civilian population little mercy; millions of them were shot.

In recent years, evidence has emerged that Soviet citizens also died as a result of compulsory deportation to the east by their own government. Some areas, such as the Ukraine and the Baltic States, welcomed the Germans as liberators from Soviet oppression. To prevent further support for Germans, Stalin moved huge numbers of Soviet people living in areas of doubtful loyalty to the east where they could not undermine the war effort. In the process an estimated 500,000 of them died from the hardships they had to endure.

ZHUKOV (1896–1974)

Zhukov was born Georgy Konstantinovich and joined the Russian cavalry in 1915. He won many medals in the First World War. He fought in the Civil War for the Bolsheviks and was later sent for officer training at Frunze Military Academy in Moscow.

Zhukov was placed in charge of Soviet forces fighting the Japanese in Manchuria in 1939. During the Second World War he fought a famous campaign to save Moscow from the Nazis. He was promoted to Marshall and received the German surrender in Berlin in 1945.

◀ A Soviet poster from 1943 showing a young woman captured by the Germans. The words say: 'Our hope is in you Red Warrior'. In the background prisoners are being shot.

Source D

ВСЯ НАДЕЖДА НА ТЕБЯ, КРАСНЫЙ ВОИН!

During the Second World War the Soviet Union, the United States and Britain had been allies against Germany, Italy and Japan. But even before the war ended cracks began to appear in the alliance. Stalin was convinced his allies had not fought hard enough to help the Soviet Union. He believed that the western powers were quite happy to see Germany overrun his country because that would weaken it, making it easier to dominate after the war. He knew that the west hated communism. After 1945 he took steps to ensure that the Soviet Union was well defended against future attack.

The Red Army had liberated much of eastern Europe and the Soviet Union was extremely popular. Stalin took advantage of the fact that his army was in occupation to annex (take over) Estonia, Lithuania, Latvia, Finland and parts of Poland. Some territory was also taken from Germany, for example East Prussia, which was then peopled with Russians. He also helped ensure that Communist governments were elected in Czechoslovakia, Hungary, Poland, Bulgaria and Romania. Now the Soviet Union had a defensive 'buffer zone' between itself and the western powers.

The western powers, led by the United States, viewed these actions in a different light. They were convinced that the Soviet Union wanted to spread its political beliefs across the globe. They saw Stalin's actions as aggressive, not defensive. As early as 1946, the former British Prime Minister, Winston Churchill had made a speech talking of how the Soviet Union had drawn an 'Iron Curtain' across Europe. President Truman of the United States agreed and promised American help to any country trying to resist Communism. In 1949, the North Atlantic Treaty Organization (NATO) brought the United States and most of western Europe together a military alliance. In response, the Soviet Union formed its own Communist alliance, the Warsaw Pact. For the next forty years the two sides fought a **cold war** against each other. This was a war of words and propaganda as east and west tried to discredit each other. Relations between them were now dominated even more by suspicion and distrust than they had been before the war.

Source F

A shadow has fallen across the scenes so lately lighted by the Allied victory. From Stettin on the Baltic to Trieste on the Adriatic an iron curtain has descended across the continent ... whatever conclusions may be drawn from these facts – and facts they certainly are – this is certainly not the liberated Europe we fought to build up. Nor is it one which contains the essentials of permanent peace.

▲ Winston Churchill speaking at Fulton, Missouri in the United States in March 1946.

▼ Soviet gains in eastern Europe 1945.

Soviet gains in eastern Europe 1945–9

Stalin died in March 1953. His body was put on display in the Kremlin and thousands of Soviet citizens turned up to pay their last respects. Many wept openly in the street at the news of his death. Yet such was the control that the Stalinist government had over the Soviet people that it is very difficult to know exactly what they thought of their leader. There must have been millions of people who hated Stalin, but who could not express their views. Criticism of Stalin was simply not allowed. There was also a conscious effort by the government to promote the 'cult of Stalin'. Pictures and statues of Stalin appeared all over the country, books, newspapers and films had to show positive images of him and schools, hospitals and towns were named after him. Consequently, most of the contemporary criticism which we have of Stalin comes from foreign writers and artists.

Source 2

Soviet policeman: 'What do you think of the government, comrade?'
Soviet citizen (playing it very carefully): 'About the same as you do, comrade.'
Soviet policeman: 'In that case I've got to arrest you, comrade.'

▲ A joke from the Soviet Union during Stalin's leadership.

▼ A French cartoon from 1935. The caption says 'We are perfectly happy'.

Source 1

SOMMES BIEN HEUREUX

Nikita Khrushchev, who succeeded Stalin as Soviet leader in 1953, made strong criticisms of Stalin's leadership in a speech in 1956. His speech was followed by a policy of **de-Stalinization**. Stalin's economic policies were criticized and millions of political prisoners were released from labour camps. Censorship was also relaxed and books such as Ilya Ehrenburg's *The Thaw* suggested that the Soviet Union was entering a more liberal era after the harshness of Stalin's rule.

In Chapters Six and Seven, we have looked at the most important of Stalin's policies. Many of them, such as the Five Year Plans, collectivization and Stalin's work during the war, provide evidence which can be used to criticize or praise Stalin. Other policies, particularly the purges, are less easy to interpret from both sides. But what about the day-to-day lives of the individual Soviet people? Apart from having to be careful about what they said and being driven to meet high production targets, how did Stalin's rule affect them?

FACT FILE

1 Stalin insisted that all Soviet people should be given a free education. He said that it was the duty of all children to acquire knowledge so as to be 'of the greatest possible service to the country'. By 1950 almost all those aged under 50 and over 8 could read and write.

2 Stalin reversed the policy of divorce on request and made abortion a criminal offence. Tax benefits were given to large families. By this policy Stalin hoped to increase the birth rate.

3 Large numbers of hospitals were built and thousands of doctors were trained. There were more doctors per head of the population in the Soviet Union than in Britain. There was free health care for all.

4 Rebuilding and new housing projects were started after the war. Flats in apartment blocks were provided for families, though there was still a housing shortage.

5 Russian workers were given holidays with pay, insurance against accidents at work and pensions when they retired.

6 Stalin relaxed Lenin's measures against the Orthodox Church, because of its support during the war. Thousands of churches were allowed to re-open.

Source 3

Stalin was a very distrustful man, sickly suspicious ... This created in him a general distrust even towards party workers whom he had known for years. Everywhere and in everything he saw 'enemies', 'two-facers' and spies. When Stalin said that one or another should be arrested, it was necessary to accept on faith that he was an 'enemy of the people' ... Suffice it to say that from 1954 to the present time the military section of the Supreme Court has rehabilitated 7,679 persons, many of whom were rehabilitated posthumously.

Stalin, using all conceivable methods, supported the glorification of his own person. In various ways he tried to convince the people that all the victories gained by the Soviet Union during the war were due to his courage, daring and genius – and no one else. Not Stalin, but the Party as a whole, the Soviet government, our heroic army, its talented leaders and soldiers, the whole Soviet nation – these are the ones who won victory in the war.

Comrades! We must abolish the cult of Stalin decisively, once and for all.

▲ Extracts from a speech made by Khrushchev to the Communist Party's Twentieth Congress in 1956.

What did the Soviet people gain from Stalin's rule?

The Soviet Union under Stalin was a country with very few liberties for the people. Stalin developed a cult of the personality, whereby his image appeared in the press and on almost every street corner. The message that was given was that Comrade Stalin was the Soviet Union and the Soviet Union was Comrade Stalin. No criticisms of the leader were allowed and opposition was rigorously suppressed. Under such a system it was impossible to make an objective assessment of what Stalin contributed to the Soviet Union.

Following Stalin's death he was denounced by his successor Khrushchev and is now considered by many historians to have been little more than a ruthless megalomaniac, desperate to hang on to power. It is now unfashionable to see any good in Stalin's rule.

The sources on these pages provide additional evidence to the text of Chapter 7, to present a more balanced account of life in the Soviet Union under Stalin. The reader must make up his or her own mind about whether Stalin's rule benefited or harmed the people of the Soviet Union.

30838